The Complete UNOFFICIAL Guide to The Sopranos Seasons I and II

By: Kristina Benson

The Complete Unofficial Guide to the Sopranos: Seasons I and II

ISBN: 978-1-60332-045-0

Edited By: Brooke Winger

Copyright© 2008 Equity Press. No part of this publication may be reproduced, stored in a retrieval system, or transmitted in any form or by any means (electronic, mechanical, photocopying, recording or otherwise) without either the prior written permission of the publisher or a license permitting restricted copying in the United States or abroad.

The scanning, uploading and distribution of this book via the internet or via any other means without the permission of the publisher is illegal and punishable by law. Please purchase only authorized electronic editions, and do not participate in or encourage piracy of copyrighted materials.

Equity Press is not affiliated with HBO, Home Box Office, HBO subsidiaries, A&E, its creater David Chase, any HBO writers or directors.

Trademarks: All trademarks are the property of their respective owners. Equity Press is not associated with any product or vender mentioned in this book.

Printed in the United States of America

Table of contents

Symbols, Signs, and Themes 13
Dreams 13
Other Aspects of the Series 14

The Episode Guide 15

Season One 17
"The Sopranos—Pilot Episode" 18
   Guest Stars and Notable Appearances 18
   Synopsis 18
   Symbolism 23
   Hits 23
   Trivia 23
   Thematic Elements 26

"46 Long" 27
   Guest Starring 27
   Synopsis 27
   Symbolism and Thematic Elements 30
   First Appearances 31
   Hits 31
   Trivia 31

"Denial, Anger, Acceptance" 33
   Guest Starring 33
   Synopsis 33
   Symbolism and Thematic Elements 36
   First Appearances 36
   Hits 36
   Trivia 37

"Meadowlands" 39
   Guest Starring 39
   Synopsis 40
   Symbolism and Thematic Elements 42
   First Appearances 42
   Hits 42
   Trivia 43

"College" 45
    Guest starring 45
    Synopsis 45
    Symbolism and Thematic Elements 47
    Hit 48
    Trivia 48

"Pax Soprana" 51
    Guest Starring 51
    Synopsis 51
    Symbolism and Thematical Elements 53
    First Appearances 53
    Hits 54
    Trivia 54

"Down Neck" 55
    Guest Starring 55
    Synopsis 55
    Symbolism and Thematic Elements 56
    First Appearances 56
    Trivia 57

"The Legend of Tennessee Moltisanti" 59
    Guest Starring 59
    Synopsis 60
    Symbolic and Thematic Elements 63
    First Appearances 64
    Trivia 64

"Boca" 67
    Guest Starring 67
    Synopsis 68
    Thematic Elements and Symbolism 69
    Trivia 70

"A Hit is a Hit" 71
    Guest Starring 71
    Synopsis 71
    Thematic Elements 74
    First Appearances 74
    Hits 74
    Trivia 75

"Nobody Knows Anything" 77
   Guest Starring 77
   Synopsis 77
   Symbolism and Thematical Elements 79
   First Appearances 79
   Hits 79
   Trivia 79

"Isabella" 80
   Guest Starring 80
   Synopsis 80
   Symbolism and Thematical Elements 82
   Hits 83
   Trivia 83

"I Dream of Jeannie Cusamano" 84
   Guest Starring 84
   Synopsis 85
   Hits 89
   Trivia 90
   Symbolism and Thematic Elements 90

Season Two 91
   "Guy Walks Into a Psychiatrist's Office" 92
      Guest Starring 92
      Synopsis 93
      First Appearances 96
      Hits 97
      Trivia 97

   "Do Not Resuscitate" 99
      Guest Starring 99
      Synopsis 99
      First Appearances 102
      Hits 102
      Trivia 103

   "Toodle Fucking-Oo" 105
      Guest Starring 105
      Synopsis 105
      First Appearances 108
      Trivia 108
      Symbolic and Thematic Elements 109

"Commendatori" 111
    Guest Starring 111
    Synopsis 111
    First Appearances 114
    Hits 115
    Trivia 115

"Big Girls Don't Cry" 117
    Guest Starring 117
    Synopsis 117
    Trivia 120

"The Happy Wanderer" 121
    Guest Starring 121
    Synopsis 122
    First Appearances 124
    Hits 125
    Symbolism and Thematic Elements 125
    Trivia 125

"D-Girl" 127
    Guest Starring 127
    Synopsis 127
    Trivia 130

"Full Leather Jacket" 133
    Guest Starring 133
    Synopsis 133
    Hits 136
    Trivia 136

"From Where to Eternity" 137
    Guest Starring 137
    Synopsis 137
    Hits 139
    Trivia 139

"Bust Out" 141
    Guest Starring 141
    Trivia 143

"House Arrest" 145
    Guest Starring 145
    Synopsis 145

"The Knight in White Satin Armor" 149
    Guest Starring 149
    Synopsis 150
    First Appearances 152
    Hits 153
    Trivia 153

"Funhouse" 154
    Guest Starring 154
    Synopsis 155
    Hits 157
    Trivia 157

Introduction

The Who's Who

Anthony "Tony" Soprano (James Gandolfini) is the boss of the DiMeo crime family, and patriarch of the Soprano household. The series begins with an anxiety attack that motivates him to start going to therapy. His therapist, referred to him by his next door neighbor and physician, is Dr. Jennifer Melfi, a competent professional who soon finds herself struggling to negotiate the very thin line that separates her responsibilities to her patient from her wariness of getting too involved in Tony's life. There are several times when she doesn't walk this line carefully enough, and is threatened by Tony, and by his enemies.

Tony's immediate family consists of his wife Carmela Soprano (Edie Falco), daughter Meadow Mariangela Soprano (Jamie-Lynn Sigler) and son Anthony "A.J." Soprano, Jr. (Robert Iler). Carmela, as the series progresses, experiences increasing distress over Tony's infidelity and life as a mobster. This distress however, is countered with her penchant for enjoying the riches and privileges that come from being the wife of a Soprano mob boss. Throughout the season, she struggles with the mental turmoil she experiences as a result of disliking Tony's business while still wanting to benefit from it. A.J. is initially a typical adolescent, struggling with an unconfirmed diagnosis of ADHD and teenage rebellion. Meadow is a gifted student who, like her mother, is sometimes unable to succesfully ignore her father's business, and hopes to pursue a career in either law or medicine.

Tony's extended family includes his mother Livia Soprano (Nancy Marchand), sisters Janice Soprano (Aida Turturro) and Barbara Soprano Giglione (Nicole Burdette), uncle Corrado "Junior" Soprano (Dominic Chianese), cousin Tony Blundetto (Steve Buscemi) and "nephew" Christopher Moltisanti (Michael Imperioli).

Dr. Melfi surmises that Tony's relationship with his mother may be partially responsible for his panic attacks, and governs the nature of his relationships with most women. Junior has seniority over Tony in their criminal empire and strives to maintain power, often straining the relationship with his nephew Tony as a result. Janice, who has had a child in Quebec, ran off to Seattle at a young age, but returns to New Jersey decades later and becomes involved in a disruptive relationships with some of Tony's colleagues. Barbara has moved away to start her own family. Blundetto grew up with Tony, but was convicted of armed robbery in their youth. Christopher is Carmela's second cousin, but Tony considers him his nephew and protege.

Tony's close circle within the DiMeo crime family includes Silvio "Sil" Dante (Steven Van Zandt), Peter Paul "Paulie Walnuts" Gualtieri (Tony Sirico) and Salvatore "Big Pussy" Bonpensiero (Vincent Pastore). Sil is Tony's consigliere and best friend, Paulie and Big Pussy are longtime crew members who have worked with Tony and his father. Also in Tony's crew are Patsy Parisi (Dan Grimaldi) , Furio Giunta (Federico Castelluccio) and Carlo Gervasi.

Other significant characters in the DiMeo family include Bobby "Bacala" Baccalieri (Steven R. Schirripa), Richie Aprile (David Proval), Ralph Cifaretto (Joe Pantoliano), Eugene Pontecorvo (Robert Funaro) and Vito Spatafore (Joseph R. Gannascoli). Bobby is a subordinate of Junior's, who eventually becomes involved with Janice. Cifaretto is ambitious to the point of making life difficult for Tony. Richie Aprile is released from prison in season two and immediately causes problems.

Symbols, Signs, and Themes

Dreams

Tony has vivid dreams in which his real life troubles manifest themselves. He dreams of a perfect mother figure, of clown houses, of informants turning into fishes. His dreams often express his fears and desires, and force him to confront issues that he is able to put in the back of his mind when awake.

Animals

Tony has a deep connection with most animals, contrasting his lack of lasting relationships with most humans. In his first session with Melfi, he worries excessively over the presence of a duck family in his pool, and dreams of waterbirds. Melfi theorizes that the ducks represent his family, and the dreams emote his fear of losing his family. Throughout the season, animals play a key role in Tony's dreams.

Mob Movies

The people depicted in the Sopranos are aware that Hollywood cinema has a rich history making films about Italian American mobsters, and often refer to films such as Goodfellas, Casino, and, of course, The Godfather.

Other Aspects of the Series

In the series, the viewer is exposed to a level of character development that is usually not possible in TV series. Because the episodes are an hour long, and there are roughly 12 per season, the writers and actors are given a rare opportunity to explore nooks and crannies of their lives and psyches.

Tony, the central figure in the show, finds himself in the dilemma of being forced to get in touch with his feelings. His willingness to continue therapy is interesting and begs certain questions; after all, a mobster with feelings probably won't make a particularly effective one. Tony's position in the mafia calls for him to lie, cheat, steal, and kill, and his quest for self-realization is very much in conflict with those aspects of his job.

Though he makes progress in therapy, and takes Dr. Melfi's suggestions seriously, he is still not able to really see all of the contradictions in his life, at least, not by the end of season one. Still, his journey is productive, and the viewer is able to use his therapy sessions as a vehicle for understanding his life.

The Episode Guide

Season One

"The Sopranos—Pilot Episode"

Guest Stars and Notable Appearances

- Jerry Adler as Hesh Rabkin
- Michael Santoro as Mahaffey
- John Ventimiglia as Artie Bucco
- Kathrine Narducci as Charmaine Bucco
- Joe Lisi as Dick Barone
- Drea de Matteo as Adriana La Cerva
- Bruce Smolanoff as Emil Kolar
- Joe Pucillo as Beppy Scerbo
- Siberia Federico as Irina Peltsin (pilot only)
- Michael Santoro as Father Phil Intintola (pilot only)

Synopsis

New Jersey mobster Tony Soprano becomes sweaty, winded, and faints while manning the BBQ prior to his son's birthday party. After going through a battery of physical assessments and tests, his collapse is diagnosed as being a panic attack, and he's referred to psychiatrist Jennifer Melfi for treatment. In their first meeting, they discuss the events that lead up to his anxiety attack and subsequent collapse.

Although Tony dutifully arrives on time for his appointment, he is initially uncooperative, detailing profound scorn for mental health practitioners and the institute of psychiatry in general. He tells her he is a 'waste management consultant' and elaborates on by saying he has a feeling that he has come in at the end of something, and that he yearns for times past and old friends. Tony tells Dr. Melfi a story about a family of ducks landing in his pool and nesting there. Hehas been stressed at home lately since his daughter is hanging out with a friend—Hunter Scangarello— that his wife regards as a bad influence, and later mentions that there has, recently, been a lot of friction between his wife and his daughter. Tony also tells Dr. Melfi about the stress of teaching his "nephew" Christopher the family business and acting as his mentor.

After Dr. Melfi warns him that she has to go to the authorities only under very certain circumstances, they are able to establish the ground rules of what will fall under doctor-patient confidentiality. So Tony feels comfortable being honest about broad aspects of career, but keeps the violent details under wraps.

Tony talks about the stress he has taken on in caring for his aging mother, Livia, who is an unending pessimist, and manages to be demanding and self-deprecating incessantly. He also mentions his wife's close relationship with her priest, Father Phil Intintola, as a minor stress. By the end of their first session Dr. Melfi succeeds in making Tony admit he may feel depressed but he leaves in a huff when she presses him to talk more about the ducks.

Later, Tony tries to coax his mother into living at a retirement community called Green Grove, but is treated to a vituperative diatribe wherein she details her desire to die right then and there. This in turn prompts a second panic attack. Tony returns to Dr. Melfi and she prescribes him Prozac, which he uses as an excuse to ditch their next appointment. He runs into her at Vessuvio, however, and covertly praises the effects of the medication, telling her that he is impressed with the "decorating tips" she gave him. Dr. Melfi's date is impressed by Tony's ability to get them a table immediately, despite the fact that the hostess had warned them of a long wait.

At their next session Tony continues to deny the challenges he's currently facing with depression and panic. He attributes his good mood to the the medication but Dr. Melfi tells him it cannot be the medication, as it takes six weeks to work and feels that their work in therapy is responsible for his improvement. Tony describes a dream where a seagull steals his penis, and from this, Dr. Melfi explains to Tony that he may have projected his love for his family onto the family of ducks living in his back pool. Tears well up in his eyes. She tells him that their flight from the pool sparked his panic attack and made him face his fear of somehow losing his own family.

At dinner with his wife at the same restaurant where he ran into Dr. Melfi with his mistress on his arm, Tony confesses to Carmella that he is taking Prozac and seeing a psychiatrist. Carmella, who thought that Tony was going to confess to adultery, is happy and tells Tony that she is proud of him. Tony really tries to hammer home that he only told her because she is the only one he is absolutely honest with, but she treats this information with contempt and disbelief.

Tony's nephew Christopher kills Emil Kolar, heir to the Czechoslovakian waste management company that rivals the Sopranos', in the backroom of Satriale's pork store by shooting him in the head three times. Originally planning to dump the body in a Kolar family garbage dumpster as an example, Christopher instead defers to the wisdom of longtime family soldier "Big Pussy" Bompensiero, and buries the body. The burial is effective; The Kolars drop their rival bid following the disappearance of Emil.

Tony begins a new enterprise inspired by his MRI scan. Mahaffey, a compulsive gambler who owes money to Tony, is intimidated into making false claims to pay out to the organization in order to cover his debts. Herman "Hesh" Rabkin, a family friend, advises Tony on this scheme and of some problems with his Uncle Junior, who feels jealous of Tony's high status in the organization.

Tony's Uncle Junior wants to rub out Little Pussy Malanga in Artie Bucco's restaurant, Vesuvio. Tony, however, is childhood friends with Artie, and worries that a mob hit in could ruin Artie's business. When Tony approaches Junior, he flatly refuses to execute the to hit anywhere else. Artie's wife demands that Artie reject Tony's offer to leave town for a weeklong cruise, so Tony, while at their daughters' soccer game, instructs his right-hand man Silvio Dante to detonate an explosion in Artie's restaurant, hoping that Artie can collect insurance money without sullying himself with gang land contact.

At a birthday party Tony and his crew try to comfort Artie about losing his restaurant, and Tony offers his eternal help. Chris storms off, and when Tony presses him he learns that Chris feels he should have gotten more accolade for his input on the Triborough Towers garbage conflict and his execution of Kolar. Tony then tells Chris that he himself was mentored and parented without compliments or support, and then Chris brags about script offers from Hollywood. Tony loses his temper breifly and grabs him, however, his good mood returns shortly.

While giving Livia a ride to AJ's rescheduled birthday party, an embittered Junior muses about eliminating Tony if he continues to interfere in his business. Tony's mother's reaction is just to silently look the other way.

Symbolism

- Tony plans out a hit at his daughter's soccer game, highlighting the way his mob life overlaps with that of his family life

Hits

- Emil Kolar, a Czech mobster who is shot by Christopher

Trivia

- This is the only episode to be directed by David Chase.

- Tony mentions his admiration for Gary Cooper, one of the many references to classic Hollywood.

- Christopher references Luca Brasi, the enforcer from "The Godfather" whose death was announced when it was said he "sleeps with the fishes". Pussy attempts to make Christopher understand that not every situation can be resolved by sending messages with violence, establishing a trend throughout the series where the younger generation has unrealistic expectations for their profession, often influenced by pop culture.

- Carmella and Father Phil discuss "The Godfather" movies and we learn that Tony prefers II because of the scenes in Sicily.

- Adriana La Cerva, portrayed by Drea De Matteo, is actually credited as "Hostess" in this episode before receiving her name later.

- Irina is played by Siberia Federico and Father Phil is played by Michael Santoro. These roles are recast with Oksana Babiy and Paul Schulze in forthcoming episodes.

- Dr Bruce Cusamano - Tony's neighbour and family physician is referenced in this episode and he makes his first appearance later in the season in the episode "A Hit is a Hit"

- In this episode, the pork store the guys use as a meeting place is Centanni's Meat Market, a real butcher shop in Elizabeth, New Jersey. However, because the shop had a steady business and because local business owners were annoyed with the incidental effects of having a "movie" production being shot on a weekly basis, HBO acquired an abandoned location in Kearny, New Jersey and renamed the pork store Satriale's Meat Market for use in future episodes.

- When describing Uncle Junior, Tony tells Dr. Melfi that his uncle embarrassed him by telling all his girl cousins he didn't have the makings of a varsity athlete.

- Carmela wants to take Meadow to the Plaza Hotel for a family tradition. Though Meadow declines in this episode, viewers finally see it take place in the season four episode, Eloise.

- Tony's ownership of JFK's sailing hat that he keeps on the Stugots is established in this episode - he later shows it off in the season 5 episode "In Camelot"

- Joe Lisi, Michael Santoro, John Ventimiglia and Jerry Adler are all listed as guest stars in the opening credits of this episode.

- Christopher calls Junior "Uncle Junior" when he greets him. This is inconsistent with how he refers to him for the rest of the show's run.

- Tony insists on calling Green Grove a "retirement community" throughout the episode - this becomes a running joke on the show.

- Tony says that anyone would think he was "Hannibal Lecture" before he started therapy - a reference to the famous fictional cannibal and also one of the first examples of a character uttering a malapropism or mispronouncing a word. The technique becomes a recurring device on the show both as humour and a device to show the lack of education of the mobsters.

- The song displayed over the end credits is "The Beast in Me" by Nick Lowe

- AJ's birth date is revealed in Kaisha as July 15th, making this episode take place in the summer. But, Hunter is picking Meadow up for school, which would be out of session during that time.

Thematic Elements

Tony's mob life and his family life are intertwined, as we see in this episode. Tony discusses business at his daughter's soccer games, and invites gangsters to his son's birthday party. The extent to which he can wear the mask of an effective father and an effective gangster is a huge element of the series.

"46 Long"

"46 Long" is the second episode of the first season of the HBO original series, the Sopranos. The episode was written by David Chase and was directed by Dan Attias. It originally aired on Sunday January 17, 1999.

Guest Starring

- Michael Rispoli as Jackie Aprile
- Anthony DeSando as Brendan Filone
- Drea de Matteo as Adriana La Cerva
- Al Sapienza as Mikey Palmice
- Sharif Rashed as Antjuan
- J.D. Williams as Special K
- Manny Siverio as Hector Anthony

Synopsis

Brendan Filone and Christopher have embarked on a partnership together, hijacking trucks, and a recreational relationship that consists of doing speed and going to clubs. They hijack a shipment of DVD players from a Comley Truck and do the driver a favor, beating him up so he won't be accused of being in cahoots with them. They deliver the DVD players to Tony, Silvio and Paulie at the Bada Bing where Tony makes it clear that he is not impressed with Brendan, mostly because he doesn't like Brendan's meth habit.

Chris and Brendan's activities infuriate Uncle Junior, who is actually being paid to protect the Comley Trucking vehicles. After Uncle Junior has a sit-down with acting boss Jackie Aprile, Sr. and Tony Soprano, he complains vociferously about Chris and Brendan, and it is revealed that Jackie has cancer and is pondering over naming his successor. When Tony leaves, Junior complains to Mikey about the way Tony treats Livia. Later, at Satriales, Tony relays Junior's message to Chris. Chris complains to Tony that he is due to be made after his efforts on the Tri Borough towers garbage disputes. Brendan offends Tony by insulting Jackie and Tony throws him out. Tony takes Chris' 15,000 dollar tribute and pockets his cut with a promise to talk Junior down.

Brendan and Chris, both high on speed, plan another hijacking on a delivery of Italian suits. However, when Brendan comes by to pick up Christopher, he learns that his partner is not going to participate in this particular gig. Christopher, though reluctant to go, doesn't succeed in deterring Brendan, who is still high. Brendan then recruits Antjuan and Special K to execute the plan. Things don't go as smoothly this time: when the truck driver is threatened, he steps out of the truck. Special K drops his gun and the driver is accidentally killed by the stray bullet. The would-be hijackers flee from the scene.

Chris tells Tony about what happened, and though Brendan tries to cover for Christopher, Tony is still angry. He tells Chris and Brendan that they must return the truck to Comley and restitution must be made after he and his crew help themselves to a small number of suits.

Pussy and Paulie, meanwhile, are sent to find out who stole Anthony Junior's science teacher's car. They are able to find the perpetrators but not the car and order the perpetrators to steal a new one in its place. The car is then painted and parked in the spot where the it as the old car had been stolen from. The teacher, at first thrilled, becomes confused as to why the paint is still wet, the interior is a different color, and the key is different despite the presence of identical plates.

After Livia accidentally sets her kitchen on fire while sauteeing mushrooms, Carmela offers to have Livia come live with her family. Livia rejects the idea and becomes distraught about the loss of her husband, a "saint". Tony hires a Trinidadian nurse to take care of her but the nurse eventually quits the job. Tony asks why and Livia dismissively tells him that you never know with "these blacks".

Livia drives her friend Fanny home and accidentally goes forward and runs her over when she goes to reverse out of her driveway. Her doctors say she can't live alone any more and Tony places Livia in the Green Grove retirement community. While visiting her house to pack up her things Tony is overcome by another panic attack.

Tony's therapy continues and he discusses his mother with Dr. Melfi. We learn that he is feeling guilty about not being able to have his mother live with them. Melfi reminds Tony of Livia's difficult relationships with all of her children, and the lack of happy childhood memories. Tony, however, still blames Carmela for preventing his mother living with them and refuses to hold his mother responsible. In another session Melfi pushes Tony to admit he has feelings of anger towards his mother, even that he hates her, and he storms out.

Georgie the barman at the Bada Bing is confused about the operation of the telephone system, and Tony vents his anger by beating him with a telephone handset.

Symbolism and Thematic Elements

- Tony is torn between his wife and his mother, two of the most important women in his life

- Tony is unable to express anger towards his mother, and instead projects it onto others, beating the barkeep at the Bada Bing. Displacement of anger is a key challenge that Tony grapples with throughout the season.

First Appearances

- Jackie Aprile, Sr., Acting Boss of DiMeo Crime family. Meets Tony and Uncle Junior at Satriale's to discuss his cancer and his current position.

- Brendan Filone, Christopher's friend and partner in crime. He is rather reckless but he is well aware of Tony's influence and hopes to somehow move up in the ranks alongside Christopher.

- Georgie, Barman at the bada bing who upsets Tony

- Mikey Palmice, Uncle Junior's consigliere and trigger man who Tony dislikes.

Hits

- Hector Anthony, killed when Brendan Filone's henchman, Special K, drops his gun by accident.

Trivia

- This is the only episode that features a teaser scene before the opening credits.

- Michael Rispoli is credited as a guest star in the opening credits

- The first episode to feature Silvio's Al Pacino impression

- The first episode to feature Tony beating up Georgie, the Bada Bing bartender

- This episode shows Tony's practice of driving to payphones to talk business matters, a practice featured in many mob movies. In the series, they refer to the practice as "calling from an outside line".

"Denial, Anger, Acceptance"

Guest Starring

- Michael Rispoli as Jackie Aprile, Sr.
- Anthony DeSando as Brendan Filone
- Jerry Adler as Hesh Rabkin
- Sharon Angela as Rosalie Aprile
- Michelle de Cesare as Hunter Scangarelo
- Oksana Lada as Irina Peltsin
- Drea de Matteo as Adriana La Cerva
- Al Sapienza as Mikey Palmice

Synopsis

Christopher and Brendan Filone return the truck they stole to Comley Trucking, but Junior is not satisfied. Junior and Mikey figure out what their options are in terms of dealing with Brendan and Christopher.

Silvio approaches Tony on behalf of a Hasidic hotel owner named Shlomo Teitlemann. Teitlemann and his son meet with Tony until the son eventually gets angry and storms out. He wants Tony to persuade his daughter's husband to grant his daughter a divorce with no compensation, and in turn, he will give 25 percent of his business to Tony. This is would work out well for everyone except the son-in-law, because the son-in-law wants 50 percent. Paulie and Silvio accost Ariel, the son-in-law, but are unable to convince him to walk away from the marriage and the hotel with nothing.

During a second encounter, they seek help from Tony, and Ariel dares the men to kill him, believing his death will bring spiritual harm to his father-in-law. He references the Masada, site of a long siege between a small number of Jew and legions of Roman soldiers. The siege ended in the mass suicide of the Jews who preferred death to enslavement. He concludes the story by asking "and the Romans—where are they?" to which Tony answers "you're looking at 'em." Ariel, however, still is not agreeing to the deal. After taking Hesh's advice to threaten Ariel with castration, Ariel agrees to the divorce. Shlomo then tries to give Tony cash instead of his original offer of 25%, because he believes he had more part in negotiating the solution. When Tony insists on the original 25% arrangement Shlomo says he has created a golem; when Tony asks what that means, he calls him a Frankenstein.

In therapy Tony discusses acting boss Jackie's cancer. The crew visits Jackie in the hospital where he is being cared for by his wife Rosalie. Tony later returns with a dancer from the Bada Bing so Jackie can enjoy a private party. On a third visit, Jackie has gotten worse and he is unable to focus on business. Tony discusses Jackie's downturn and the insult from Shlomo—that he's a golem--with Dr. Melfi. She asks him if he feels like he has no feelings, like a monster.

Carmela organises a silent auction at the Soprano home to raise money for a pediatric hospital. She recruits Charmaine and Artie

Bucco to cater the event while visiting their new home. Tony and Artie bicker after Tony tells Artie to stop whining about the fire in his restaurant. Carmela offends Charmaine by treating her like a servant. Later, Charmaine gets her back by revealing that she and Tony once slept together.

Meadow and Hunter are stressed out becuase the SATs and their choir recital fall on the same day, and they don't have enough time to both practice enough and study enough. They decide that they can get everything done if they are able to get some speed Christopher and Brendan. Christopher, at first reluctant, decides that it's better they get it from him than from street dealers and agrees to give it to Meadow "just this once".

Junior visits Livia at Green Grove and discusses the Christopher and Brendan situation. Livia points out that both she and Tony love Christopher like a son and suggests Junior give Tony's hot-tempered nephew a "talking to", but says that she "doesn't know" about Brendan. Junior is grateful for her advice but she remarks that she must be "a babbling idiot" for Tony to put her in a nursing home.

The "talking to" given to Christopher is given is a mock execution at the hands of Russian goons. They fire an empty gun into his head and leave him on the dock, having wet his pants. Junior's trigger man, Mikey Palmice, puts a bullet through Brendan's eye while he's in the bathtub. Both scenes are interspersed with Meadow's recital, allowing the lullaby All Through the Night to provide a backdrop for the violence.

Symbolism and Thematic Elements

- Once again, Tony's role as a father overlaps with his role as a mobster when we see Christopher and Brendan punished while listening to his daughter's choir

- The title of the episode refers to the five stages of grief and appears to foreshadow Jackie's death

- Tony's role as a husband and a mobster again interfere with eachother when one of his lovers tells his wife they slept together

- Chris tells Meadow he will sell her drugs to keep her from going to street dealers because they would rob her and leave her on the side of the road. This may be foreshadowing.

First Appearances

- Rosalie Aprile, wife of acting boss Jackie Aprile and friend of Carmela Soprano

Hits

- Brendan Filone, shot in the eye while in his bathtub by Mikey Palmice.

Trivia

- The juxtaposition of the singing of Meadow's choir and the killing of Brendan is similar to the baptism sequence in The Godfather when Michael has his enemies killed during the christening of his nephew.
- Denial, anger and acceptance are three of the Five Stages of Grief described by Elizabeth Kubler-Ross in her 1969 book <u>On Death and Dying</u>
- With Tony as a co-owner, the Teitlemann hotel is seen many times throughout the series.
- The closing song in this episode is "Complicated Shadows" by Elvis Costello.
- Ariel references Masada. In actuality, only one of the Jews committed suicide. Because Judaism strongly discourages suicide, the defenders were reported to have drawn lots and slain each other in turn, down to the last man, who would be the only one to actually take his own life.
- At one point, Tony is called a golem. A golem is a yiddish word with a few possible meanings. It can refer to anything that is incomplete or in an embryonic stage, or an entity made from inanimate matter, it can mean monster, or it can simply mean "fool".

"Meadowlands"

"Meadowlands" is the 4th episode of the HBO original series, The Sopranos. It was the 4th episode for the show's first season. The episode was written by Jason Cahill and was directed by John Patterson. It originally aired on January 31, 1999.

Guest Starring

- Anthony DeSando as Brendan Filone
- Al Sapienza as Mikey Palmice
- Jerry Adler as Hesh Rabkin
- Michael Rispoli as Jackie Aprile, Sr.
- Sharon Angela as Rosalie Aprile
- Michelle de Cesare as Hunter Scangarelo
- Drea de Matteo as Adriana La Cerva
- Oksana Lada as Irina Peltsin
- John Heard as Detective Vin Makazian
- Joseph Badalucco Jr. as Jimmy Altieri
- Tony Darrow as Larry Boy Barese
- George Loros as Raymond Curto

Synopsis

Tony gets more and more paranoid about his secret meetings with Dr. Gelfi, particularly after he almost runs into Silvio Dante, who was visiting the dental office just opposite Dr. Melfi's. However, Tony is not entertainng any thoughts about quitting theray. He has developed some feelings for Dr. Gelfi, even asking one of the crooked detectives on the payroll, Vin Makazian, to follow her and take pictures of her. Unfortunately, Makazian assumes Melfi is a mistress of Tony's, and when he sees Melfi with a date, he pulls them over, conducts a field sobriety test, beats the man, and demands of a confused Melfi: ``You got prime rib at home, and you're going out for hamburger?``. At this point, Tony considers quitting therapy, scared that his crew will find out, but Carmela insists he continue, warning him that his marriage is at risk unless he keeps going. It should be noted, however, that Carmela is under the impression that Dr. Gelfi is a man.

Anthony Junior is confused when a bullying classmate, Jeremy Piocosta, backs down from a fight with him although Jeremy is much bigger. AJ comes to realise that Jeremy was intimidated by his father's reputation. It turns out that Tony had coincidently met Jeremy's father the day before at a nursery as Tony was seeking pesticide for his corn.

Christopher, sporting a neck brace from his mock execution, is terrified. He does not feel much better when he and Adriana find Brendan Filone lying dead in his bathtub, shot through the eye.

Convinced that Tony shot Brendan because he found out that Christopher sold drugs to Meadow, he feels better after he talks to Meadow and ascertains that she didn't tell her dad about the drug sale. However, finding that Junior is responsible, and that he has also assumed collection of protection money owed to Tony's crew, Chris aches for revenge, implying that he will take out Mikey Palmice. Mikey is a made guy, so Tony convinces Christopher to hang back, and instead, Tony takes a ride to the luncheonette, beats Mikey, and staples his suit with a staple gun. He then confronts Junior about what he did to Brendan and Chris.

Although Tony rebukes his nephew, he's wary about going to war with Junior, especially after Jackie's death creates uncertainty over who will be his successor as boss over the DiMeo family. Although Tony has the backing of the other capos, and is angry over what was done to Christopher, he ultimately strives for a peaceful resolution with his uncle, and after some advice Dr. Melfi about giving the elderly the ``illusion of control``, Tony concedes leadership of the family to Junior. This works to his favor because he can avoid heat from the feds since he wont be the official boss, avoid a war, still make money, and get contracts as payment from Junior in exchange for the recomendation and backing. Content with his decision, Tony opts to remain in therapy.

Symbolism and Thematic Elements

- It is possible that Christopher was merely giving the illusion of control to Tony when his complaints motivated Tony to go beat Mikey and staple him?
- The title of the episode refers to a spot in New Jersey that is notorious for being a dumping ground for the victims of Mafia violence. Who is being dumped there, metapohically speaking? Jackie? Brendan?
- Again, Tony's family is affected by his mob connections, as when AJ is spared a fight with a much bigger boy at school.

First Appearances

- Vin Makazian, A corrupt detective in the Essex County police force on Tony's payroll
- Larry Boy Barese, Jimmy Altieri, Raymond Curto, Capos in the DiMeo/Soprano crime family.

Hits

- Jackie Aprile, Sr. (cancer)

Trivia

- The Meadowlands is a region of New Jersey reputed for being a dumping ground for New York and New Jersey's Mafia murder victims.

- Big Pussy refers to Brendan Filone's execution style slaying as a 'Moe Greene special'. Moe Greene, a character in the Godfather, was hit via a bullet through the eye.

- Tony Darrow also appeared in Goodfellas as Sonny Bunz.

- Christopher quotes Al Pacino's iconic lines from the finale to the 1983 Gangster film "Scarface".

"College"

"College" is the 5th episode of the HBO original series, The Sopranos. It was the 5th episode for the show's first season. The episode was written by Jim Manos, Jr. and series creator David Chase and was directed by Allen Coulter. It originally aired on February 7, 1999.

Guest starring

- Paul Schulze as Father Phil Intintola
- Tony Ray Rossi as "Frederick Peters"/Fabian "Febby" Petrulio
- Oksana Lada as Irina Peltsin

Synopsis

Tony and Meadow drive to Maine so Meadow can visit some of the colleges that she is considering. On the drive, Meadow point-blank asks him if he is in the mafia and he, of course, denies everything. Meadow, however, is clearly not buying the ruse, and finally, Tony tells her that a portion of his income is from illegal gambling. Meadow admits to taking speed to study for SATs, but refuses to tell him where she got the drugs.

Later in their drive, Tony spots Fabian Petrulio at a gas station. Petrulio was a member of DiMeo crime family who ratted them out to the FBI and was then placed in the witness protection program. Despite the fact that the fruit of his loins is in the front seat of the car, panicking, Tony chases Petrulio through oncoming traffic, leaves his underage daughter off at a bar to get drunk with people she met that are students at a college to which she is applying, and endeavors to locate the man, confirm his identity, and wipe him out.

He confirms Petrulio's identity but fails to realise that his investigation was noticed, and Petrulio follows Tony and Meadow back to the hotel where they are staying. He aims at Tony's back as Tony is helping Meadow into the hotel, but his luck runs out, when the presence of bystanders prevents him from shooting.

The next morning, Tony drops Meadow off for an interview at Bowdoin College, and heads to Petrulio's travel agency, strangling him with wire as Petrulio pleads for his life. On his return to pick up Meadow, Tony is unsettled by the lack of trust and the fear that his daughter is clearly displaying, and is further unnerved by a Nathaniel Hawthorne quote at the college that says,d "No man... can wear one face to himself and another to the multitude, without finally getting bewildered as to which one may be true."

Meanwhile, back in New Jersey, Carmela has been at home recovering from a bad case of the flu, and watches movies and drinks wine with Father Phil while AJ is at a sleepover. The evening takes a decidedly downward turn, however, when Dr. Melfi phones to reschedule Tony's appointment, revealing to her that Tony's psychiatrist is not, as she had believed, a male. Carmela first informs Dr. Melfi that she can't take down her number since she lost her pencil "up Tony's ass", and considers kissing Father Phil, but his stomach is acutely disagreeing with the wine, and he throws up. He sleeps it off until morning on the sofa. Tony and Meadow return the same day, and after she tells Tony that Phil spent the night on the sofa, he becomes angry until to she turns the tables on him when she mentions that Dr. Jennifer Melfi called.

Symbolism and Thematic Elements

- Although Tony's life as a father has overlapped with his role as a gangster in past episodes, this is the first time that one directly undermines his ability to successfully engage in the other. Because of Meadow, he had to wait to execute the rat. Because he saw Petrulio, however, he leaves his underage daughter at a bar, with strangers, after driving dangerously with her in the front seat of his car. This may lead one to suspect that Tony identifies more clearly with himself as a mobster than as a father.

- The Nathanial Hawthorne quote is, of course, obvious. The masks that Tony wears are gradually melding together, and he is having a harder time wearing just one at once.

Hits

- Fabian "Febby" Petrulio:,strangled with a piece of wire by Tony.

Trivia

- James Manos Jr. and David Chase received the Emmy for Outstanding Writing for a Drama Series for their work on this episode.

- The college locations and the Maine scenes were filmed in rural New Jersey at Drew University in Madison, New Jersey.

- The murder of Febby Petrulio is the first time viewers see Tony killing anyone.

- James Gandolfini and Jamie-Lynn Sigler both have said that this is one of their favorite episodes.

- In an interview on the first season DVD, David Chase says that when HBO first read the script, they did not like the murder scene. Executives said that Chase had done so well in building Tony up as a protagonist that that if Tony committed such a cold blooded killing, fans would turn on him. However, Chase said that he believed fans would turn on Tony if Tony didn't complete the execution.

- Tony asks if Meadow's friends think he is cool because of The Godfather, she reply by commenting that most people she knew were bigger fans of the film Casino.

- This is the episode submitted by Edie Falco for the 51st Annual Primetime Emmy Awards. With it, she won the first of three Emmys for Outstanding Lead Actress in a Drama Series.

"Pax Soprana"

"Pax Soprana" is the 6th episode of the HBO original series, The Sopranos. It was the sixth episode for the show's first season. The episode was written by Frank Renzulli and was directed by Alan Taylor. It originally aired on Sunday February 14, 1999.

Guest Starring

- Jerry Adler as Hesh Rabkin
- Vince Curatola as Johnny Sack
- John Heard as Detective Vin Makazian
- Paul Schulze as Father Phil Intintola
- Al Sapienza as Mikey Palmice
- Tony Darrow as Larry Boy Barese
- George Loros as Raymond Curto
- Oksana Lada as Irina Peltsin
- Joe Badalucco as Jimmy Altieri
- Christopher Quinn as Rusty Irish

Synopsis

A Soprano has finally become the boss of the DiMeo Crime family, and it's Tony's Uncle Junior. However, Junior is not respecting old arrangements. He modifies old deals and tries to have more money directed into his pockets, while allowing less to run downstream down to his capos. Tony had allowed Junior to become boss in the hope that he would be able to be the acting boss while leaving Junior to deal with the difficulties associated with management. The captains share Tony's irritation, and they eventually complain to Tony about Junior's penchant for "eating alone" since he doesn't share enough wealth.

Livia convinces Junior to tax Tony's business associate Hesh, even though Hesh's arrangement was secured decades ago. When Hesh threatens Tony that he'll leave the area because of the new deal, Tony partners with Johnny Sack, a capo of one of New York's Five Families, and helps Hesh and Sack present a somewhat misleading proposition for Junior. Tony had figured out the nuts and bolts of this idea on his own, but he allowed Junior to think he was in charge, still echoing Dr. Melfi's advice to give an illusion of control.

After more persuading from the other capos, Tony meets with Junior in an attempt to motivate him to share more of the income. Using anecdotal evidence about Augustus Caesar and a dirty story about cows, Tony is successful. Junior decides to divide the money he received from Hesh and give it to his capos, and Tony returns his share to Hesh himself.

Even though Tony really controls the family, Junior is the one on the FBI's radar screen. At a banquet to honor the new Boss, the feds are there, though disguised as servers, and gathering evidence on miniature cameras. With this information, they decide to regard Junior as Jackie's replacement but Tony's position as "captain" remains the same.

Tony is facing challenges with his libido with both his wife and his mistress, and realizes that he is thinking of Dr. Melfi. At his session he professes his love for Dr. Melfi but his feelings are not returned. Carmella expresses jealouly towards Melfi, recognizing that Melfi is not just another floozy. Carmella tells Tony that she wants to be the woman in his life that is helping him, and Tony agrees.

Symbolism and Thematical Elements

- The title of this episode means Soprano Peace. Peace was gained by several parties in this episode. Tony talks to Junior and the ending result pacifies the other captains. Tony and Carmela make a step towards achieving peace in their relationship. Hesh and Tony make peace over the arrangement that had been secured ages ago and then violated.

- The episode's title also refers to a period of peace in the Roman Empire called Pax Romana. This peace resulted in part from the generosity of Caesar Augustus.

First Appearances

- Johnny Sack, a Captain the Lupertazzi Crime Family located in New York

Hits

- Dominic, Grandson of Uncle Junior's tailor who committed suicide after taking cocaine he bought from Rusty Irish.

- Rusty Irish, murdered by Mikey Palmice for selling drugs to children

Trivia

- Pax Soprana translates to "Soprano peace" in Latin.

- The title is also a reference to the period in Roman history known as "Pax Romana" which spans over a hundred years of peace in the Roman Empire. Caesar Augustus receives credit for starting this period of tranquility as the beginning of the era which coincided with his declaration ending Roman civil wars.

- The song played during the final montage and end credits is an instrumental version of "Paparazzi" by Xzibit.

"Down Neck"

"Down Neck" is the 7th episode of the HBO original series, The Sopranos. It was the seventh episode for the show's first season. The episode was written by Robin Green & Mitchell Burgess and was directed by Lorraine Senna Ferrara. It originally aired on Sunday February 21, 1999.

Guest Starring

- Joseph Siravo as Johnny Boy Soprano
- Rocco Sisto as Young Junior Soprano
- Laila Robbins as Young Livia Soprano
- Madeline Blue as Young Janice Soprano
- Bobby Boriello as Young Tony Soprano

Synopsis

Anthony Jr. and his friends steal sacramental wine from his Catholic school-Verbum Dei-- and are caught when they show up drunk to Gym Class. Tony and Carmela are called in to see the principle and the school psychiatrist, who tells them that AJ may have Attention Deficit Disorder, and that AJ may be placed in a Special class as a result.

For some reason, this leads Tony to talk to Dr. Melfi about his own childhood when he first learned about his family's Mafia ties. Included in Tony's memory is the time his father wanted to move the family to Reno, Nevada, to manage a supper club for Rocco. Tony's mother said she would rather suffocate the children than move. Tony, visiting Livia, asks her how Rocco is doing and she responds that Rocco is a multimillionaire. Tony asks her about her vehement refusal to move, and she denies not only that the move was a serious option, but also that she was involved in the decision to stay.

AJ, as punishment for getting drunk at school, is forbidden to watch TV or play Nintendo. He also has to visit his grandmother, Livia, at Green Grove every day. During one of these visits AJ discusses his possible learning disorder and tells Livia that Tony is seeing a psychiatrist.

Symbolism and Thematic Elements

- AJ's school is called "Truth of God" in Latin. This is interesting, because in a way, the episode deals with the accuracy of Tony's memory about his childhood.

First Appearances

- Johnny Boy Soprano, Tony's deceased father
- Young Janice Soprano, Tony's older sister who appears as a child in flashbacks.

Trivia

- Down Neck refers to the portion of the Passaic River in Newark, New Jersey that doubles back around a peninsula of land between Lister Street and the Pulaski Highway.

- Down Neck is the name of the section of Newark where Tony and his family live and his father does business.

- This is the first episode to feature flashbacks to Tony's childhood.

- Jefferson Airplane's "White Rabbit" plays over the end credits.

- Although the flashbacks are set in the 60's, some modern day cars are visible in the background in some of the scenes.

- During one of his flashbacks, as Little Tony watches his father rough up Rocco on the street.

"The Legend of Tennessee Moltisanti"

"The Legend of Tennessee Moltisanti" is the 8th episode of the HBO original series, The Sopranos. It was the 8th episode for the show's first season. The episode was written by David Chase and Frank Renzulli and was directed by Tim Van Patten. It originally aired on Sunday February 28, 1999.

Guest Starring

- # Anthony DeSando as Brendan Filone
- # Joe Badalucco, Jr. as Jimmy Altieri
- # Tony Darrow as Larry Boy Barese
- # Drea de Matteo as Adriana La Cerva
- # George Loros as Raymond Curto
- # Joseph R. Gannascoli as Gino
- # Will McCormack as Jason La Penna
- # Frank Pando as Agent Grasso
- # Richard Romanus as Richard LaPenna
- # Al Sapienza as Mikey Palmice
- # Matt Servitto as Agent Harris
- # Bruce Smolanoff as Emil Kola

Synopsis

At the wedding of Larry Boy Barese's daughter, Larry Boy informs the DiMeo Crime Family members that the FBI is going to begin handing out indictments to New Jersey associates who participate in mob activity. The Capos wonder about whether or not it would be prudent to take a break from business, but Junior is opposed to the idea since they will lose out on a lot in the long term .Junior becomes further agitated when there is what he perceives as too much interest in Tony's opinion. Tony agrees with Junior and reaffirms Junior's authority, and implies that Junior would want everyone to engage in some spring cleaning. The Capos then get their families together and get rid of any evidence they might have in their possession.

Tony and Carmela promptly remove cash and guns from the loft spaces but Carmela is annoyed and hurt when she has to turn over her jewelry as well. Meadow, picking up on the nature of this spring cleaning, instructs A.J. to delete the porn from his computer so the FBI won't find it. Meanwhile, Pussy burns all of his papers in a barbecue grill and Silvio tells Christopher and Georgie to search for bugs at the Bada Bing.

Tony asks Carmela to take Livia out for brunch so that he can hide the money and guns in her apartment at the retirement home. He packs some hatboxes and clothing storage acoutrements with weapons and cash. The following day, Junior visits with Livia, and she tells him what AJ had told her—that Tony is seeing a psychiatrist.

Tony tells Dr. Melfi he may not be at the next appointment because he may be going "on vacation". Dr. Melfi manages to connect the dots since there it had been on the news that the Soprano family may be indicted. In fact, Melfi's ex husband knows she has an Italian mobster patient, but does not know the patient is Tony Soprano. He is irate that the Mafia have given millions of Italian Americans a bad name, but Melfi's son points out that mobster movies have become an icon of American Cinema, and later, Melfi points out that despite his activism on behalf of Italian Americans, he still has a penchant for blonde Irish girls.

Tony does indeed miss the next appointment because the FBI has arrived at his house with a search warrent. The FBI agent, Dwight Harris, knows that he has children and does not want to upset them by being overly aggressive or forceful. They take AJ's computer and a few items of Carmela's, and everyone seems to be playing nicely together. However, tensions arise when Agent Grasso accidentally breaks a glass bowl in the Soprano kitchen, and Tony curses him in Italian. Carmela refuses to clean up the broken glass and Grasso is made to sweep the pieces off the floor. Later, over dinner, Tony complains that Italians are unfairly targeted by the police, and points out the Meucci, an Italian, invented the telephone. After a tense moment where Meadow asks who invented the Mafia, AJ says he learned that Alexander Graham Bell invented the telephone but Tony disputes this, saying everyone knows that Meucci was the real inventor of the telephone.

At his next appointment Dr. Melfi tells Tony that he will still be charged for the missed session and throws cash at her, swears, calls her a glorified hooker, and walks out of the office.

Christopher, meanwhile, is having nightmares about the man he killed, Emil Kolar. In the dream, . Emil warns him that he left evidence from the murder, and Christopher serves Emil cold cuts from a severed hand in Satriale's. The dreams permeate into his waking state and, Christopher worries about Emil's body, asking Georgie to help relocate it.

In addition to worrying about being caught for murder, Christopher is trying to write a screenplay based on his experiences in the Mafia, annoyed that he has only written 19 pages when a typical script should be 120. He also complains that his movie lacks an 'arc' to advance the characters, and also wonders if his life lacks a significant event that causes him to change his direction.

Adriana, Paulie and Pussy all try to offer support, but Christopher becomes more and more depressed. He becomes even more agitated when he sees on the news that Brendan Filone is receiving more recognition as a deceased Soprano "associate" than he is as a live one. Tony calls Christopher to drive over to the Bing to search for bugs and asks him to pick up some pastries on the way. Christopher takes his frustration out on a bakery clerk and shoots him in the foot, saying "it happens" when the clerk screams in pain.

Although upset because Christopher acted recklessly, Tony is somewhat sympathetic, and feels that he is going through something reminiscent of his own depression. He tentatively engages in Melfi-style approaches to get Chris to open up, but Chris is just confused and annoyed. The next day, Christopher's mother tells him that his name is featured in a Star-Ledger article on the Mafia. Excited, he drives to the nearest newspaper dispenser and pulls an entire stack, dropping coins in his haste to open the machine.

Symbolic and Thematic Elements

- Even though Tony threw the cash at his psychiatrist, it is clear in his discussion with Christopher about his depression that he has come to value and internalize some of the lessons he has learned in therapy.

- Possible foreshadowing: Chris complains that his life lacks a significant event. Tony tells Chris he is trying to get arrested.

- Again, Tony's role in his family is affected by his life in the crime family when he has to take his wife's jewelry from her because he has no receipts, and when his son's computer is confiscated.

- It is interesting that Tony is complaining that the police target Italians, when he himself has dived headfirst into the typical stereotype of Italian Americans, choosing to become a mobster.

First Appearances

- Agent Grasso: an agent investigating the DiMeo crime family
- Agent Harris: an agent who specializes in the DiMeo crime family
- Jason LaPenna: Dr. Melfi's son
- Richard LaPenna: Dr. Melfi's ex-husband
- Jimmy Petrille: capo in the Lupertazzi crime family.

Trivia

- Christopher is trying to write a screenplay and Adriana calls him her own Tennessee Williams, a playwright who wrote A Streetcar Named Desire.

- *When Tony scolds Christopher over the bakery incident, he tells him that this is how cowboys act.

- Christopher shoots the bakery owner in the foot. This could be a reference to the character (Michael "Spider" Gianco) which Michael Imperioli plays in Goodfellas. Spider was shot in the foot by Joe Pesci's character because he didn't bring drinks fast enough.

- Joseph R. Gannascoli who plays Gino, the bakery customer in this episode will return in Season 2 as Vito Spatafore, a soldier in the Aprile crew. Gannascoli and Dan Grimaldi are the only two actors to play two roles in the series.

- Pussy and Silvio have different wives in this episode - neither actress had any lines and are not credited for their appearance.

- This is the first episode directed by Tim Van Patten, a regular director on the series.

- Paulie references Ernest Hemingway when talking about "the guy with the bullfights, blew his head off".

- The closing song is "Frank Sinatra" by Cake.

"Boca"

"Boca" is the 9th episode of the HBO original series, The Sopranos. It was the ninth episode for the show's first season. The episode was written by Jason Cahill and Robin Green & Mitchell Burgess and was directed by Andy Wolk. It originally aired on Sunday March 7, 1999.

Guest Starring

- Candace Bailey as Deena Hauser
- Joe Badalucco, Jr. as Jimmy Altieri
- Tony Darrow as Larry Boy Barese
- Michelle DeCesare as Hunter Scangarello
- John Heard as Detective Vin Makazian
- Cara Jedell as Ally Vandermeed
- Kevin O'Rourke as Coach Don Hauser
- Robyn Peterson as Roberta "Bobbi" Sanfillipo
- Richard Portnow as Attorney Harold Melvoin
- Al Sapienza as Mikey Palmice
- Jackie Tohn as Heather Dante

Synopsis

Meadow's soccer coach Don Hauser has become well-liked by the fathers of kids in his team, and Tony, Silvio and Artie have drinks with him at the Bada Bing club after yet another win. Soon, however, they learn from the Star-Ledger that he is leaving for another job, and begin working on him to stay. Paulie Walnuts delivers a 50-inch television to the coach's house and insists he accept it, and Christopher takes the coach's dog and then returns it in a ploy for gratitude.

Meanwhile, the girls on the team are unsettled because the coach is having a sexual relationship with Ally Vandermeed, one of his players, and a friend of Meadow's. Ally tries to kill herself after she hears that the coach is leaving, and Meadow, concerned, tells her parents about their relationship.

Junior Soprano visits Boca Raton for a weekend with Bobbi, his mistress of 16 years. Bobbi feels that Junior is extremely talented at oral sex but Junior wants her to keep this on the down low because he feels it would damage his reputation in the DiMeo crime family. Bobbi, however, has already gossiped about his skills at the nail parlor, and asks her aesthetician to keep it a secret. The aesthetician, however, gossips about this to an acquaintance of Carmela Soprano, who in turn tells Tony. When Junior makes fun of Tony's golfing skills, Tony makes thinly veiled jokes about going for sushi and fish swimming down south, aimed at his activities with Bobbi. Junior, in turn, makes fun of Tony for going to therapy, and later breaks up with Bobbi, his lover of 16 years, by mashing a lemon meringue pie in her face.

After Tony learns that the coach has slept with a student, he tries to figure out whether or not he should murder him. Dr. Melfi asks him why he would assume the burden of righting wrongs in society, and later, it is revealed that the Coach is arrested. After learning of the coach's arrest, Tony comes home drunk and on Xanax, and brags to Carmela that "[He] didn't hurt no one." This statement is overheard by Meadow, who is eavesdropping.

Thematic Elements and Symbolism

- Bocca is the Italian word for mouth. Gossip and secrets are a major theme in the episode, as well as Junior's talent in cunnilingus.

- Tony's indignation at the coach's relationship with a player also reveals a certain amount of cognitive dissonance in terms of the way he feels about women, as well as his moral compass in general. This is womanizer and a philanderer who once dropped off his underage daughter at a bar alone so he could take steps towards killing an FBI informant. Yet he wants to murder a man who slept with one of his daughter's colleagues.

- Further cognitive dissonance is revealed when Tony announces proudly that he didn't hurt anyone. A sound moral compass and a turn-the-other-cheek attitude are not exactly assets to Mobsters.

Trivia

- Boca Raton is the holiday destination of choice for Junior Soprano and he visits it during the episode.

- This episode wrongly reports the location of the University of Rhode Island, claiming that it is in Providence when, in fact, it is on the other side of the state.

- Actor Steven Van Zandt wore his own golfing hat for a scene where Silvio plays a round of golf

- Junior also reportedly hides out in Boca in a flashback sequence in the later episode "To Save Us All From Satan's Power"

"A Hit is a Hit"

"A Hit Is a Hit" is the 10th episode of the HBO original series, The Sopranos. It was the tenth episode for the show's first season. The episode was written by Joe Bosso and Frank Renzulli and was directed by Matthew Penn. It originally aired on Sunday March 14, 1999.

Guest Starring

- Jerry Adler as Hesh Rabkin
- Nick Fowler as Richie Santini
- Bryan Hicks as Orange J
- Oksana Lada as Irina
- Saundra Santiago as Jeannie Cusamano
- Robert LuPone as Dr. Bruce Cusamano
- Bokeem Woodbine as Massive Genius

Synopsis

Paulie, Christopher and Big Pussy kill a drug dealer in a hotel room as a warning to his organization to stay away from Soprano territory. They steal a lot of cash from the escapade and Carmela feels that some of the cash should be invested legitmately.

Later, Tony gives Dr. Bruce Cusamano a box of Cuban Cigars to thank him for his referral to Dr. Melfi. In turn Dr. Cusamano invites Tony to play golf with him and friends at the private club of which Bruce is a member. Although initally reluctant, he end sup accepting the invite. At the subsequent barbeque with Dr. Cusamano and his friends, Carmela receives a stock tip from one of the wives, and invests in the company. The company splits 3-for-1 and Carmella is pleased.

Tony, however, comes to regret agreeing to play golf with Cusamano when the other players keep asking him to tell them about being a mobster. Tony discusses the incident in therapy with Dr. Melfi, and how he felt used for the amusement of others, much like his high school friend with a cleft palate. Ultimately, Tony avenges himself by filling a package with sand and asking Dr. Cusamo to hold on to it. Cusamo is unnerved and Tony chalks up a win for himself.

Christopher and Adriana go to the theatre in New York, and after the show, Christopher makes racist comments about the clientele surrounding them at a hot dog joint. Massive Genius - a rap star –happens to be there and is angry about the comments, and violence almost ensues. The fight fizzles out, however, when a cop tells Massive's friend Orange J that Christopher is kind of hooked up with the Sopranos. Massive decides instead to tell J to invite Chris and Adriana to a party at his home, and Adriana, recognizing Massive, asks Christopher to take her to the party. At the party, Adrianna muses about becoming a music producer, saying she has lots of experience listening to music, and mentioning that her ex-boyfriend Richie Santini is the singer in a band called Visiting Day. Christopher agrees to put up the money for her to produce a demo for them.

Richie, however, is a recovering drug addict, and has lived at home due to an extended convalsecent period stemming from an injury sustained while trying to use a downed power line to grill a fish. The session goes slowly and the producer and Richie often argue. Christopher even hits Richie with a guitar and demands he shoot crank so they can continue. Christopher takes the demo to Hesh, who has a history in the music business, and Hesh tells him that the band is not very good. Massive, however, claims to be impressed but he seems more interested in Adrianna than the music. Christopher later tells Adrianna he thinks that the only reason Massive G is encouraging her is because he wants to get into her pants. Adrianna becomes angry and storms out of their apartment.

Later, Massive G gets in touch with Hesh through Christopher. He tells Hesh that he is a relative of an artist Hesh worked with and claims Hesh owes him $400,000 in royalties since he's the dead artist's next of kin. When Hesh refuses to pay, Massive responds with a threat of litigation. Hesh mentions a countersuit over unauthorized sampling by Massive G's label of music that Hesh still controls, and the issue is left unresolved.

Thematic Elements

- In a prior episode, there was a lot of talk about the way that the cops can be racist towards Italians, however, Christopher has no problem with being racist towards blacks.

- This also reveals that Tony travels in relatively closed circles, and mostly interacts with other mobsters. Hence, he is surprised that his lifestyle might prove fascinating to members of his neighbor's country club.

First Appearances

- Dr. Bruce Cusamano: Soprano family physician and next door neighbor

- Jean Cusamano: Wife of Dr. Cusamano and friend of the Soprano family.

Hits

- Juan Valdez:,Shot in the forehead by Paulie Walnuts

Trivia

- "A Hit is a Hit" is some what of a duble entendre. Hesh says it when discussing Visiting Day's demo with Christopher.

- This episode reveals that Hesh has a penchant for African-American women

- The song played in one of the closing scenes, which Hesh hears and then says to Christopher "Now that is a hit", is "Nobody Loves Me But You" by Dori Hartley.

"Nobody Knows Anything"

"Nobody Knows Anything" is the 11th episode of the HBO original series, The Sopranos. It was the eleventh episode for the show's first season. The episode was written by Frank Renzulli and was directed by Henry J. Bronchtein. It originally aired on Sunday March 21, 1999.

Guest Starring

- Joe Badalucco Jr. as Jimmy Altieri
- Johann Carlo as Bonnie DiCaprio
- Giancarlo 'John' Giunta as Kevin Bonpensiero
- John Heard as Vin Makazian
- George Loros as Raymond Curto
- Sal Ruffino as Chucky Signore
- Michele Santopietro as JoJo Palmice
- Al Sapienza as Mikey Palmice
- Karen Sillas as Debbie

Synopsis

Big Pussy Bonpensiero and Jimmy Altieri are arrested at a pool hall belonging to Jimmy, and the FBI discovers that a pool table conceals a stash of guns. Pussy later claims he hurt his back during the chase and his subsequent capture.

Vin Makazian, a police detective on the payroll that owes Tony money, meets Tony near a harbor and tells him that he has a rat in his crew. Vin thinks it is Big Pussy Bonpensiero, but it is later revealed that Vin owed Pussy $30,000, so Tony is unable to trust his objectivity. Tony asks Vin to provide a copy of the police report naming the informant, but before he can produce it, he is arrested at a brothel, alongside Soprano family capo Ray Curto. When released, Vin commits suicide.

After Pussy is bailed out by his wife, he sits at home licking his wounds and is unable to make collections. Tony visits Pussy to let him know that Pussy has options and friends, and Pussy worries how he will put his kids through college. After the visit, Tony is unsure whether Pussy is an informant.

Tony assigns Paulie to find out for certain if there indeed is a rat in their midst but not to do anything about it unless he sees a wire with his own eyes. Paulie takes Pussy to a bath facility but Pussy refuses to undress since his doctor said heat would be bad for him. Pussy disappears after this encounter, while Tony and others are informed that Pussy's injury may be only in his head.

Jimmy is also released and comes to Tony's house, asking questions about events in the past. Tony is now confused--is Jimmy the informant? Or is it Pussy?

Junior meets with Livia, who tells him that Tony and other Capos have placed their mothers in Green Grove and have held meetings there. Junior, paranoid, still smarting from Tony's insults about Bobbi, and the underlying tension between them since Jackie's death, thinks that a plot is coalescing against him and decides to order a hit on Tony. He colludes with Mikey Palmice and Chucky Signore to organize the hit.

Symbolism and Thematical Elements

- *Trust becoming a huge issue in Tony's life. Trust with his friends, and his mother.

First Appearances

- Chucky Signore: Member of Junior Soprano's crew
- JoJo Palmice: Mikey's wife

Hits

- Vin Makazian, Jumped off a bridge

Trivia

- The episode's title refers to both Vin Makazian and Pussy Bonpensiero since Tony discovers hidden truths about two of his close friends.

- Paulie says "Nobody knows anything" referring to Pussy's back problem.

"Isabella"

"Isabella" is the 12th episode of the HBO original series, The Sopranos. It was the twelfth episode for the show's first season. The episode was written by Robin Green and Mitchell Burgess and was directed by Allen Coulter. It originally aired on Sunday March 28, 1999.

Guest Starring

- Joseph Badalucco Jr. as Jimmy Altieri
- Maria Grazia Cucinotta as Isabella
- John Eddins as John Clayborn
- Katalin Pota as Lilliana
- Sal Ruffino as Chucky Signore
- Al Sapienza as Mikey Palmice
- Paul Schulze as Father Phil Intintola
- Matt Servitto as Agent Harris
- Touche as Rasheen Ray
- David Wike as Donnie Paduana

Synopsis

At Mariolina Capuano's funeral, Jimmy Altieri tells Uncle Junior that Brendan Filone's mother was extremely upset at his funeral. Once Jimmy leaves, Uncle Junior complains to Mikey that Jimmy has loose lips about the Filone hit, and shares with Mikey that Mariolina gave him his first hand job. Why he felt the funeral an appropriate venue to share this information is not explored.

Tony sinks into a severe depressive episode, and his spirits are momentarily lifted when he sees a beautiful Italian woman named Isabella in the Cusamano's yard. Isabella tells Tony that she is a foreign exchange dental student, and guesses that Tony is from Avellino, Italy. Tony later dreams that she is breastfeeding a baby named Antonio. Later, however, we learn that Isabella was a daydream at best and a hallucination at worst. Dr. Melfi theorises that Isabella was an idealised maternal figure produced by Tony's subconscious.

Junior hires two guns from the outside- Rasheen Ray and John Clayborn - contracted through Donnie Paduana, in keeping with his goal of taking out a hit on Tony. Ray and Clayborn tail Tony and wait for him outside a store near Dr. Melfi's office. Christopher, however, is worried about Tony, and has also followed him to the store, and by sheer accident prevents the assassination attempt. Junior meets with Donnie after the first attempt fails and Donnie cracks a joke at Tony and Livia, prompting Junior to conclude that Donnie has a big mouth. Mikey then kills Donnie.

Rasheen Ray and John Clayborn, nonetheless, are not relieved of their duties, and again wait for Tony near Dr. Melfi's office. As Tony stops to buy the paper and orange juice, they open fire as Tony sees their reflection on his car door. He is hit but still is able jump into his SUV and start it. When Rasheen reaches the door Tony grapples with him and he accidentally shoots John on the other side of the vehicle. Tony pulls away, holding Rasheen through the window, finally dropping him when he is at a higher speed. Though his leg and ear are injured, Tony seems actually to have had his spirits raised by the event and his depressive behavior does not resume.

Agent Harris of the FBI visits Tony at the hospital to attempt to convince Tony and Carmela to enter the witness protection program. He claims that Tony is no longer safe on the street, but Tony dismisses the event as a carjacking, a completely random event. Silvio, Paulie and Christopher, however suspect Junior, and discuss this suspicion among themselves when Junior calls on Tony at home after Tony's release from the hospital.

Symbolism and Thematical Elements

- As Tony learns in therapy, Isabella is a desire of his manifestation to have a good relationship with his mother. It is interesting that she appears in his neighbor's yard. As we learned when he plays golf with the doctor and his wife, they have a "normal" family, and are "white bread wops". Could this be a latent longing for a life of normalcy?

- Possible foreshadowing: the FBI tells Tony that he is not safe on the street.

Hits

- Donnie Paduana, Shot by Mikey Palmice

- John Clayborn, Accidentally shot by his partner Rasheen Ray in the failed attempt on Tony Soprano's life

Trivia

- Isabella is a character in the episode, although actually being a hallucination/imaginary experience that Tony experiences.

- As Tony is about to be shot, he purchases orange juice from a vendor. In the Godfather, Don Vito Corleone barely survives an assasination attempt after buying oranges.

- The song that is played twice this episode (during the time Tony is in his bedroom) is Tiny Tears by the Tindersticks.

- The song that plays over the ending credits is "I Feel Free" by Cream.

"I Dream of Jeannie Cusamano"

"I Dream of Jeannie Cusamano" is the 13th episode of the HBO original series, The Sopranos. It was the thirteenth episode for the show's first season. The episode was written by David Chase and directed by John Patterson. It originally aired on Sunday April 4, 1999

Guest Starring

- Al Sapienza as Mikey Palmice
- Saundra Santiago as Jeannie Cusamano
- Sharon Angela as Rosalie Aprile
- Paul Schulze as Father Phil Intintola
- Joe Badalucco, Jr. as Jimmy Altieri
- George Loros as Raymond Curto
- Tony Darrow as Larry Boy Barese
- Robert Lupone as Bruce Cusamano
- Frank Pellegrino as Agent Cubitoso
- Frank Pando as Agent Grasso
- Matt Servitto as Agent Harris
- Michele Santopietro as JoJo Palmice
- Sal Ruffino as

Synopsis

At Uncle Junior's meeting with his capos, Jimmy Altieri makes it impossible for the boss not to realize that he is wearing a wire, and Junior agrees to let Tony have him killed. Christopher takes Jimmy to a hotel under the auspices of a night with two Russian broads. After they enter, Silvio comes out from behind a door and shoots Jimmy in the back of the head. His body is later found with a rat stuffed in his mouth.

Dr. Melfi, in a session with Tony, tells him that his dreams indicate his subconscious is alerting him to problems with his mother, and suggests that she may be at the center of the attempts on his life. Tony is enraged and attacks Dr. Melfi, holding her down on her chair, and telling her that not only are they finished, but she is lucky he won't hurt her for suggesting such a thing.

Meanwhile, Carmela and Rosalie Aprile have lunch at Nuovo Vesuvio's, Artie Bucco's restaurant that he opened with the insurance money from the original Vesuvio's. Father Phil drops by and sits with them, discussing the food, and the watch. The watch had originally belonged to Rosalie's husband Jackie Aprile but after his death, Rosalie had given it to Father Phil. Meanwhile, Artie's wife Charmaine complains that the old Vesuvio had been a haven for Mafia types, and now it was looking like the new Vesuvio would be as well.

FBI Agents Harris and Grasso hold a meeting with Tony and U.S. Attorney Gene Conigliaro. They play recordings that they made at Green Grove, and Tony hears Junior and Livia planning a hit on him, as well discussing Tony's visits with Dr. Melfi. The purpose of playing these tapes was to convince Tony that his days are numbered, and try to persuade him once again to join the witness protection program.

At Green Grove, while Artie Bucco visits Livia, she tells him that it was Tony that burnt down the original Vesuvio. Artie is shaken up. He later confronts Tony with a loaded rifle outside Satriale's meat market, lamenting that Vesuvio's had employed three generations of Buccos that worked over the same stove. Tony denies that he started the fire, telling his friend that Livia was confused and old, and not to be paid any mind. He swears "on his mother" that he did not burn down the restaurant, so Artie withdraws, apologizes, and smashes the rifle.

At the Bada Bing, Tony tells Paulie, Silvio and Christopher that he knows Junior took out the hit on his life. Paulie suggests that Junior may use his own staff this time to finish the job. Ergo, they decide that Chucky Signore should be made to "disappear without setting off any alarms."

Tony and Silvio meet up with Chucky at the Marina and Tony pulls a gun out of the mouth of a fish he is carrying, and shoots Chucky. Silvio unloads cement blocks and chains from the car and put them in Chucky's boat.

Tony somehow manages to convince Dr. Melfi to let him see her, and tells her she was correct about his mother. He asks her to leave town, telling her that her life could be threatened. She tries to out-logic him, explaining that Tony's enemies would have nothing to gain from coming after her, but Tony insists and she reluctantly agrees.

Artie Bucco visits Father Phil and consults him about the anger and rage he is feeling towards Tony and life. Father Phil tells Artie he should tell his wife, Charmaine, that Tony started the fire, and moreover, he should turn in Tony to the police.

Tony finally comes clean to his crew about seeing a psychiatrist, telling them he started going because of the times when he fainted. His crew is more sympathetic that he had anticipated: Silvio doesn't seem to mind, Paulie admits to once seeking similar help himself because he had issues and "lacked some coping skills." Christopher asks if it is like marriage counseling then appears upset as he gets up and leaves the meeting.

Carmela visits Father Phil and sees Rosalie and Father Phil having an intimate discussion, as Father Phil eats and praises the food that Rosalie has brought him. Carmela storms off in disgust and dumps the bowl of food she was about to give him in the trash can outside the church.

Back at the new Vesuvio, Charmaine hires Adriana La Cerva as a hostess and tells Artie that she is very happy with the new restaurant and how things are progressing. Artie then decides that it may be unnecessary to tell her about Tony and the fire.

Mikey Palmice heads out for a jog with his cellular phone, instructing his wife that she should call him on his cel if Chucky calls the house. Paulie and Christopher, the latter of whom is still aching to take revenge for the hit on Brendan Filone, track down Mikey and chase him into the woods. Christopher confronts Mikey about Brendan, while Paulie is more distracted because he thinks he got poison ivy on him. Both empty their guns into Mikey and his cell phone rings almost immediately thereafter.

The FBI arrests Junior, capo Larry Boy Barese, and underboss Joseph Sasso and 13 others. On the news, it is reported that Mikey "Grab Bag" Palmice is missing and may have fled. Tony learns from his lawyer that he was not indicted because the charges relate to a telephone stock scam that he was not involved with.

Father Phil visits Artie and Artie confesses that he never told his wife of the information concerning Tony and the fire because she seems for the first time in a long time to be happy.

Meanwhile, the FBI tries to make a deal with Junior. They tell him to say that Tony was the de facto boss of the family, running things behind Junior's back with the help of two New York families and Johnny Sack. The Feds are actually after bigger targets in New York. Junior, however, perhaps out of loyalty or perhaps out of pride, refuses.

Father Phil visits Carmela with a movie rental and asks about Tony. Carmela is resentful, pointing out that despite Father Phil's outspoken opposition to Tony's lifestyle, he sure enjoys watching Tony's fancy TV and eating his nice food, even accusing the priest of using food and sexual tension to manipulate women who are spiritually and emotionally thirsty.

Tony goes to Green Grove to confront his mother, picking up a pillow on the way to her room. But as she is being wheeled into the nursing facilities, Tony learns that she has had a stroke. He discards the pillow but tells her he knows what she has done.

As a storm erupts, Tony is driving with his family and decides to take them to Nuovo Vesuvio is located. Tony, Carmela and the children hurry to the door where Tony begs Artie to let them in so they can get out of the storm. Artie, who is cooking by candlelight without electrical power, reluctantly opens the door and welcomes them in, where they meet Paulie and Silvio. Tony proposes a toast to his family, and they enjoy dinner.

Hits

- Jimmy Altieri: Lured to a hotel by Christopher and shot through the back of the head by Silvio for possibly being involved with the FBI

- Chucky Signore: Shot by Tony in a marina for conspiring with Uncle Junior to have Tony killed

- Mikey Palmice: Chased down and shot to death in the woods by Paulie and Christopher for killing Brendan Filone, and for conspiring with Uncle Junior to have Tony killed

Trivia

- The episode's title refers to the 1960s television series, I Dream of Jeannie due to the fact that Tony has a dream about his neighbor's wife, Jeannie Cusamano.

Symbolism and Thematic Elements

- When Carmela criticizes Father Phil for his inconsistancy and duplicity, is it really herself she is criticizing? After all, she has many qualms about his lifestyle but few when it comes to using her power for her own gain.

Season Two

"Guy Walks Into a Psychiatrist's Office"

"Guy Walks Into a Psychiatrist's Office" is the 14th episode of the HBO original series, The Sopranos. It was the first episode for the show's second season. The episode was written by Jason Cahill and was directed by Allen Coulter. It originally aired on Sunday January 16, 2000.

Guest Starring

- Lillo Brancato Jr. as Matthew Bevilaqua
- Chris Tardio as Sean Gismonte
- Jerry Adler as Hesh Rabkin
- George Loros as Raymond Curto
- Suzanne Shepherd as Mary De Angelis
- Tom Aldredge as Hugh De Angelis
- Aida Turturro as Janice Soprano
- Ed Vassalo as Tom Giglione
- Oksana Lada as Irina Peltsin
- Dan Grimaldi as Philly "Spoons" Parisi
- John Fiore as Gigi Cestone
- David Margulies as Neil Mink

Synopsis

Several months after Mikey Palmice's execution and Livia's hospitalization,. Tony begins to self-medicate and has not been visiting Dr. Melfi on a regular basis. Dr. Melfi, meanwhile, has had to see her clients at a motel after being warned that her office is not safe. Christopher hires another man to take his Series 7 exam in his place. Uncle Junior is in jail. Carmela continues to play housewife. Livia begins physical therapy so she can recover from the stroke. Raymond continues to bring in the money for Tony as does Paulie and Silvio. Pauli and Silvio enjoy their incomes, purchasing designer shoes and evenings with Bada Bing strippers.

Tony continues to see his Russian mistress Irina and hides the fact that he was out all night by doing a load of laundry. He then sneaks into bed and falls asleep. The following morning, as Tony goes to fetch the paper he sees a Riviera car heading toward his drive, and just as Tony begins to fear it's a driveby, Pussy emerges. Tony yells "you've been gone all these months...and this is how you come back to me!"

Tony and Pussy then go down to the basement to catch up. Pussy tells Tony that he was in Puerto Rico because of his back. He met a girl while there, so he didn't want to tell his wife, and anyway, he had no longer felt safe in New Jersey because he feared that Tony and his crew thought he was a rat. Tony still does not trust Pussy and as he goes to hug him he pats him down. Pussy becomes offended but Tony give him a genuine hug. At the Bada

Bing, the associates welcome Pussy and Silvio entertains the group with Godfather impressions and quotes.

The following day, Christopher is made the head of an investment firm and is pressuring people to push a new stock which in reality is a scam. When Christopher pretends he's going out on business but is actually out to meet Adriana, he puts Matt Bevilaqua, a fellow stockbroker, in charge. While Matt is doing his rounds with friend Sean to make sure people are advising their clients to buy the stock, they find that one broker, instead of selling what he is told, is basing his investment advice on the needs of the customer. They proceed to pour hot coffee on him and beat him. The former manager tells them to break it up but Matt threatens him to go back into his office. The following day, Tony receives a phone call from the firm stating that Christopher is not doing his job and that two people left because of an incident. Tony tells Christopher to be careful and gives him a stern warning.

Soon after, Carmela calls Tony to tell him that his sister, Janice, who he hasnt sen in years, has come around and is looking for a place to stay. Tony invites his sister to stay even though he is well aware that when she leaves he will be "$5000 lighter". Tony suggests to Carmela that they have a big family reunion with Tony's other sister Barbara and all of the children. Livia, however, is not welcome.

While driving, Tony has a panic attack and runs off the road. Scared and worried, he meets with another psychiatrist but the doctor tells Tony that he recognizes him, and has seen Analyze This, and that he is not taking new clients at this time.

Tony tells Janice that he doesn't want to hear his mother's name ever again in his house. His sister responds that she will continue to see Livia and possibly vacate her house but Tony tells her that he will be selling the house. Later, Tony and Carmela are informed by a realtor that Livia's house was vandalized.

Carmela then asks when he is getting back into therapy and tells Tony that her parents will be coming to the party as well since Livia won't be there. In the past, her parents and Tony's mother had not gotten along, and they had avoided events where Livia would be present. She asks him about when he will be getting back into therapy.

At the party, Carmela notices that Tony doesn't seem to be having a good time, and asks him when he will be getting back into therapy. Tony tells her that he does not know but that he has been self-medicating. Meanwhile, Janice and Barbara are talking about the way Tony is handling everything. Janice thinks that no one is going to get their fair share from the house but Barbara believes otherwise.

Tony orders a hit on Philly "Spoons" Parisi, an active soldier in the Junior Soprano crew who has been spreading rumours that Tony tried to suffocate his own mother with a pillow. Tony assigns Gigi Cestone to do the hit, and when Gigi gets out of Philly what he knows, he shoots him in the head. Tony then decides everything is safe for Melfi, and contacts her. He tries to apologize to her over a meal at the diner, but she is extremely upset that she was uprooted from her office, and that she could not help another patient who committed suicide. Tony feels bad but ask her if he can come back, perhaps get a referral from her. She tells him to get out of her life and not to expect a referral, and he leaves the diner. Tony then goes home to have lunch with Carmela, who is surprised that he is home early.

First Appearances

- Janice Soprano (also known as Parvati Wasatch): Tony's sister who has resurfaced after a 20 year absence while living in Seattle.

- Barbara Soprano Giglione: Tony's younger sister who lives in Brewster, New York.

- Matt Bevilaqua and Sean Gismonte: Stock brokers at Christopher's firm who are looking get themselves some recognition by the Soprano family.
- Gigi Cestone: a soldier in the Junior Soprano crew.

- Neil Mink: Tony Soprano's attorney and confidante

Hits

- Philly "Spoons" Parisi, killed by Gigi Cestone for spreading rumors that Tony likes to "fluff his mother's pillows".

Trivia

- The episode's title is intended to be the beginning of a joke (for example, Guy walks into a bar).

- Dan Grimaldi, who plays Philly "Spoons" Parisi in this episode will go on to play Patsy Parisi (Philly's twin) in future episodes.

- Aida Turturro (Janice Soprano) and Drea de Matteo (Adriana La Cerva) are now billed in the opening credits.

"Do Not Resuscitate"

"Do Not Resuscitate" is the 15th episode of the HBO original series, The Sopranos. It was the 2nd episode for the show's second season. The episode was written by Robin Green & Mitchell Burgess and Frank Renzulli and was directed by Martin Bruestle. It originally aired on Sunday January 23, 2000.

Guest Starring

- Lillo Brancato Jr. as Matthew Bevilaqua
- Chris Tardio as Sean Gismonte
- Bill Cobbs as Reverend Herman James, Sr.
- Steve R. Schirripa as Bobby "Bacala" Baccalieri
- Robert Desiderio as Jack Massarone
- Louis Lombardi as Agent Skip Lipari
- Richard Portnow as Harold Melvoin
- Gregory Alan Williams as Reverend James, Jr.
- John Fiore as Gigi Cestone

Synopsis

Tony meets Uncle Junior at prison, and expresses irritation that he was not on the visitor's list for two weeks. Tony tells him to be careful and that he is lucky that he is letting him earn. Junior tries to convince Tony that Livia had nothing to do with the hit but Tony doesn't believe him. He tries to talk business but Tony refuses, expressing an interest in meeting with Bobby Bacala, Junior's "courier" and soldier in his crew.

When Bobby Bacala meets Tony at the pork store, Tony tells him that Junior still holds the title of boss, and he can still "earn" via his shylock business and the pipe fitter's union, but everything else of Junior's is now his. Bobby says that he will tell Junior, but adds "to the victor go the spoils." Tony tells Bobby to shove his "book of quotations" somewhere and to get out.

The following day, Junior's lawyer Harold Melvoin gets Junior out of jail and into house arrest after convincing the judge that Junior has a recurring heart problems. The house arrest comes with a couple conditions: he is to wear a position monitoring bracelet, and he can only leave the house for grocery shopping, family functions and doctor's appointments.

Later, Junior goes to the doctor and Tony is present. This way they can talk business without violating the judge's orders for house arrest. Junior tells Tony that the owner of the Green Grove Nursing Home, Fred Capuano, has been discussing Soprano family business with others, saying that "Tony Soprano likes to fluff his mother's pillows." Shortly after, a state trooper finds Capuano's car and toupee at the side of the road.

After Pussy has surgery for his back, his friend Skip Lipari takes him home. Their conversation reveals that Pussy has been working for the FBI since 1998 and now that Jimmy Altieri is dead, Skip wants Pussy to step up and "stop being Tony's errand boy". Pussy tries to convince Skip that his loyalty is to the government, not to Tony Soprano, but nonetheless, he continues to lie to Lipari and provide him with bad intelligence about the Sopranos.

When Tony learns that Massarone Construction is being subjected to protests because they don't hire enough minorities, Tony is asked to stop the protests. Tony then sends in several mob associates to scare the protesters away from the construction site. This tactic works. In an attempt to forge a new and possibly useful ally, Tony later tries split the money he was paid to end the protests with the protest leader, Reverend Herman James. Reverend James states that his deceased father would not have liked the arrangement, but that it is a business arrangement that could not be refused.

Janice continues to visit Livia in the hospital. When Janice asks Meadow what brings Livia joy, Meadow tells her that Livia enjoys opera and show tunes. Janice then purchases a set of records and plays them for her mother. Later, Livia begins to choke but is rescued with the assistance of a nurse. The nurse then discusses with Janice whether to make Livia a "DNR" otherwise known as "Do Not Resuscitate" if she ever is comatose. Janice talks it over with Tony who advises her to do whatever she wants and that she can even move into Livia's house if she chooses so.

Anthony Jr. overhears this and asks Livia if "DNR" is the same as "DNA," as he is writing a school paper on DNA. Livia is shocked that the DNR is even on the table for discussion, and when Janice tells Livia she is ready to go home, Livia makes a snide refernce to the DNR. Livia is then brought back to her hospital room where she calls Carmela and tells her about her troubled children and how they weren't raised right, and Carmela hangs up on her, first warning her to never call the house again.

The following evening, Junior slips in the bathtub while shaving and believes that he has fractured something. Bobby Bacala then calls Tony for help and Tony hurries over to find Junior lying on the couch in his bathrobe. Tony then picks his uncle up on his shoulders and proceeds to drive him to the emergency room despite his objections.

First Appearances

- "Black" Jack Massarone, owner of Massarone Brothers Construction which was once run by Uncle Junior

- Bobby "Bacala" Baccalieri, member of the Junior Soprano crew who becomes Junior's aid

Hits

- Fred Capuano, supposedly murdered after spreading gossip about the Soprano family.
- Reverend Herman James, Sr. dies of natural causes due to old age.

Trivia

- Although the episode aired second, it was the third to be produced.

- Agent Lipari stated that Pussy has been working with the FBI since 1998 which would mean that Tony's suspicion of Pussy wearing a wire during Christmas '95 in episode 3.10 ...To Save Us All From Satan's Power was false.

"Toodle Fucking-Oo"

"Toodle Fucking-Oo" is the 16th episode of the HBO original series, The Sopranos. It was the 3rd episode for the show's second season. The episode was written by Frank Renzulli and was directed by Lee Tamahori. It originally aired on Sunday January 30, 2000.

Guest Starring

- Vince Curatola as Johnny "Sack" Sacrimoni
- Peter Bogdanovich as Dr. Elliot Kupferburg
- Paul Herman as Peter "Beansie" Gaeta
- Matthew Sussman as Dr. Schreck
- Michele de Cesare as Hunter Scangerelo

Synopsis

Richie Aprile, the late Jackie's brother, is on parole after spending ten years in prison. In his first few days out of jail, Richie visits a respected pizzeria owner, Beansie Gaeta, who was once one of his partners. Richie states to Beansie that he wants respect and that he wants what is owed to him. Beansie tells him to back off, and Richie knocks him down by hitting him in the face with a coffee pot, and then throws a chair at him and hits him several times.

Meanwhile Tony is informed by the West Orange police that his daughter Meadow threw a party at Livia's house. Not only was the house trashed, several partygoers overdosed and drugs and alchohol were found on the scene. Since the police officer owed Tony a favor he agreed not to expose what really happened at the party. When Tony confronts Meadow and Hunter on the drive home, Meadow insists that it was not her fault and that it was supposed to be a small gathering of friends. When they arrive home, Meadow just runs up the stairs when Carmela questions her. The following morning, Carmela is trying to figure out a suitable punishment. Tony replies to Carmela; "Hey let's not overplay our hand, because if she finds out that we're powerless, we're fucked!". After Meadow comes clean, she selects her own punishment by allowing her parents to take away her Discover Card.

At first after hearing about Meadow's escapades, Janice sees Meadow's relinquishing of the Discover card as a sign that she is becoming more independant. However, when Janice discovers the mess at Livia's house, including but not limited to stained walls and vomit on the hardwood floors, she thinks that Meadow is getting away with murder. Tony becomes annoyed at Janice and tells her to stop intruding on how they raise their kids. This argument culminates with Carmela advising Janice to "Mind your fucking business, keep your mouth shut when it comes to my kids!" Hurt, Janice then leaves the house.

While eating dinner at a nice Italian restaurant, Dr. Melfi shares a bottle of wine with some friends. As they finish up and leave the restaurant, Melfi sees Tony and asks how he has been. Tony says that he is fine, and asks how she has been. Melfi, it turns out, has been fine as well. She then recommends a menu item and Tony asks if they are now making small talk. Melfi then leaves, saying "toodle-oo". At a therapy session with her own therapist, Dr. Kupferberg, she says she feels annoyed because she feels that she acts differently when she is around Tony. The following night, Melfi has a dream that Tony has a car accident while reaching for a prozac tablet. As Tony crashes the car, music from The Wizard of Oz plays in the background. Melfi wakes up from her dream and writes it down in her notebook.

Tony then decides to throw Richie a "welcome home" party after his long prison term. At the party, all of Richie's debtors, except Beansie, pay him homage with envelopes of money. When Richie asks if Beansie is there, Tony tells him to lay off him. Hours after the party, Richie finds Beansie and tries to shoot him for not showing up to the party. Beansie splits, but later, underestimating how long it would take for Richie to give up and leave, he returns to his car and Richie, in the adjacent car, runs him over. Tony later visits Beansie in the hospital where his wife becomes very confrontational over his injury since the doctor says he may not ever walk again.

Tony meets Richie at the mall and relays to him that Beansie will never walk again. Richie reminds Tony that no one ever went to see him in jail, and that Beansie deserved what he got. Later, Richie sees Janice at yoga class where they begin to reminisce about their pasts. Richie then tries to win Janice over by bringing a bouquet of flowers to Livia's bedside. Over sodas, Janice tells Richie that they are both in very different places but Richie insists that they give their relationship another chance.

When Tony goes to change the locks at Livia's, he discovers Meadow scrubbing the floors and cleaning up the house as part of her punishment. Tony turns away from the house and puts his arms on his hips, clearly deep in thought. The episode ends with a closeup of his confused face.

First Appearances

- Richie Aprile, The late Jackie Aprile's brother who is paroled from prison after a 10 year sentence.

- Dr. Elliot Kupferburg, Dr. Melfi's colleague and therapist

Trivia

- The episode's title is a common form of "good-bye". Melfi adds her own twist on the saying while mulling over her run-in with Tony.

- Although the episode aired third, it was the second to be produced.

- David Proval (Richie Aprile) originally auditioned to play the role of Tony Soprano. He was turned down because David Chase felt he looked "too right" for the part.

Symbolic and Thematic Elements

- Until this episode, when Melfi admits to her therapist that she acts differently around Tony, Melfi has seemed to be the only person in his life over which Tony has no sway.

"Commendatori"

"Commendatori" is the 17th episode of the HBO original series, The Sopranos. It was the 4th episode for the show's second season. The episode was written by David Chase and was directed by Tim Van Patten. It originally aired on Sunday February 6, 2000.

Guest Starring

- Sofia Milos as Annalisa Zucca
- Federico Castelluccio as Furio Giunta
- Louis Lombardi as Agent Skip Lipari
- Toni Kalem as Angie Bonpensiero
- Sharon Angela as Rosalie Aprile
- Maureen Van Zandt as Gabriella Dante

Synopsis

While attempting to watch a bootleg version of The Godfather, Part II, Tony tells his crew that he, Paulie, and Christopher, will be travelling to Naples to make a deal with a local Camorra family (distantly related to the Sopranos) over the smuggling of stolen cars. Although Tony is looking forward to the trip, he downplays his excitement to Carmela, who is upset that Tony will go abroad with his mafia associates but not his own family. Tony tries to explain to Carmela that it is a business trip and there will not be enough time for leisure activities, but she remains skeptical and annoyed.

Over lunch with Rosalie and Gabriella, Carmela asks Angie Bonpensiero how her things are at home with Pussy now that he's back. Angie says that she has been sick every day since he got home. Angie then tells the wives that she recently undergone a test for a tumor and Pussy had little sympathy for her. She goes on to tell them that she has considered suicide but instead will get a divorce. Angie's tests soon come back negative, and she begins to file for the divorce papers as soon as the legal firms return from the Jewish holiday.

Carmela reminds Angie that Pussy is a doting father, and persuades her to stay with Pussy for the sake of their children, but Angie tells Carmela that when Pussy arrived home after many months of absence, she felt depressed and angry. When Pussy arrives home and silently presents flowers to Angie, a smile flickers on her face, but then she swats him with them.

The state of his marriage has been the least of Pussy's concerns lately; he has been burdened by the pressure of his situation as an informant, and is getting more and more paranoid by the day. Pussy is unsettled when he is spotted by Jimmy Bones, a professional Elvis impersonator and acquaintance, during a meeting with his FBI handler Agent Skip Lipari. They cover for themselves, telling Jimmy that Skip is a mob associate from Delaware. Skip insists that their cover worked, but Pussy is not convinced, and later beats Jimmy to death with a hammer as a precautionary measure.

Tony, Christopher and Paulie arrive in Naples and meet their translator, Furio Giunta. Furio then informs him that they will be dining with several capos in the Naples family and that Don Vittorio, boss of the family, will be present. Paulie and Tony go to the dinner but find that they are instead doing business with another made man, Nino, and Tony is not interested in talking to him. When they meet the Don, however, it becomes clear that Vittorio is merely a boss by title, and is senile and incapable of conducting business.

Frustrated, Tony is informed that the Don's son-in-law, Mario Zucca, had stepped in to replace him, but is in prison serving a life sentence, so Mario's wife Annalisa now controls the family. On leaving the restaurant, Tony and Paulie are shocked to see Furio and his cohorts try to get respect by brutally beating a boy who set off fireworks as the Don passed. They even punch his mother when she tries to intervene. The next day, Tony meets Annalisa, but he is not entirely comfortable with doing business with a woman, and tensions are further raised by the boss' mutual sexual attraction. Tony's companions from back home prove incapable of offering support; Christopher has spent his time locked in his hotel room with prostitutes and junkies, and Paulie has been on a mission to rediscover his roots, only to conclude that he really dislikes Neapolitan hospitality, cuisine, and plumbing.

The following day, Annalisa calls for Tony and says that they still have some unfinished business to discuss. Tony says that in order for their arrangement to work, she has to transfer Furio to his family. Annalisa won't agree, saying Furio is one of her best men. Tony offers to trade her the stolen cars at a reduced price in exchange. She agrees and they relax, visiting several city landmarks. Tension is also resolved when Tony tells Annalisa that to have a sexual relationship with a business partner would be to "shit where he eats". At Newark Airport, Pussy drives up to take them home; Paulie describes his trip as "fabulous", Tony is still brooding over his unfulfilled attraction to Annalisa, and Christopher, finally sober from his heroin daze, is busy buying Adriana a gift from the airport shop.

When Tony enters his home and announces his return home, Carmela is in her bedroom and tries to pull herself together as she goes down the stairs to see him.

First Appearances

- Furio Giunta, a made man from the Naples mob headed by Don Vittorio and Annalisa Zucca. Furio is sent to America after a successful trade between Tony and Annalisa.

- Angie Bonpensiero, Pussy's wife of 24 years who is a "mob wife" and is good friends with Carmela Soprano, Gabriella Dante and Rosalie Aprile.

- Gabriella Dante, Silvio's wife who is a "mob wife" and is good friends with Carmela Soprano, Rosalie Aprile and Angie Bonpensiero.

Hits

- Jimmy Bones, an Elvis impersonator and mafia associate who sees Pussy with an FBI agent

Trivia

- The episode's title is an Italian word for commander which is an honorable title in Italian society. Tony is given this greeting in Italy, which Paulie hears and then tries to use throughout the episode.

- Series creator David Chase is seen in the episode at an Italian patisserie where Paulie Walnuts says "commendatori" to him.

- The song "Con Te Partiro" by Andrea Bocelli is played four times throughout the episode.

- Although the episode aired fourth, it was the ninth to be produced.

- The scene where Paulie attempts to make conversation with the locals on the waterfront was not scripted; Tony Sirico was filmed interacting with passersby.

"Big Girls Don't Cry"

"Big Girls Don't Cry" is the 18th episode of the HBO original series, The Sopranos. It was the 5th episode for the show's second season. The episode was written by Terence Winter and was directed by Tim Van Patten. It originally aired on Sunday February 13, 2000.

Guest Starring

- Vince Curatola as Johnny "Sack" Sacrimoni
- Jerry Adler as Hesh Rabkin
- John Ventimiglia as Artie Bucco
- Kathrine Narducci as Charmaine Bucco
- Peter Bogdanovich as Dr. Elliot Kupferberg
- Steve R. Schirripa as Bobby "Bacala" Baccalieri
- Federico Castelluccio as Furio Giunta
- Louis Lombardi as Agent Skip Lipari
- Oksana Lada as Irina Peltsin
- John Fiore as Gigi Cestone

Synopsis

With Furio now working as a soldier for The Soprano family, Tony promotes Paulie and Silvio to capo and consigliere respectively. While dining at Nuovo Vesuvio, Tony asks Artie for a favor: to hire his "cousin" Furio from Italy as a mozzarella maker. Artie tells Tony that they have no openings on the staff at the moment, and that his wife Charmaine would not be crazy about the idea. Artie eventually, however, is assured that he will not have to pay Furio, and then agrees to give Furio a trial run until Furio can retain full citizenship.

Tony then throws a party for Furio and Pussy begins to become very jealous. Junior and Bobby show up at the party, but Carmela slams the door in their face since she suspects Junior took the hit out on Tony. Tony then gives Furio his first assignment: he must collect from husband-wife brothel owners who owe Tony money. Furio completes the job by beating both and shooting the husband in the knee.

Meanwhile, Dr. Melfi calls Tony on his cell phone. She vividly describes her dream- he was in a car crash as he desperately searches for his Prozac. She believes that the symbolism in the dream is that Tony's car accident is caused because she abandoned him. As Tony is waiting for Furio, she tells him that she has an open appointment the next day.

Christopher is enrolled in an acting class to assist him in his endeavors to write a screenplay, but soon finds that the class is demanding and its rigorous schedule overlaps with his mob life. While acting out a scene from the film Rebel Without a Cause, Christopher becomes very emotional and cries, leaving the room with embarassment even though his colleagues are clapping with genuine appreciation. During the next class, Christopher and another acquaintance practice an acting exercise and Christopher beats his partner. Christopher tells Adriana how the exercise reminded him of his father's murder and how betrayed he felt. That evening, Christopher rids himself of any traces of his unfinished screenplay, "You Bark, I Bite" by disposing of the printouts and floppy disks in the dumpster.

When Janice decides to take out a loan on Livia's house in order to renovate it, Tony is enraged. He rips a telephone out of the wall and throws it on the floor in front of AJ. Carmela sends AJ upstairs and later, Tony goes up to apologize and tells AJ lies about his temper tantrum, the most creative of which is that he is " a new product tester for Radio Shack".

Later, Tony goes to Livia's house and discovers that Richie Aprile has spent the night with Janice. Before leaving, he informs Richie that Janice is now his problem.

Later on the Stugots (Tony's boat), Tony gets mad at Irina because she is feeding Cheese Doodles to ducks swimming near the boat. Tony feels that Cheese Doodles are perhaps not the best thing for a duck's digestive system, and gets angry. Another boat owner suggests to Irina that if she does not like to fight she should find herself a Russian man. Tony then walks to the man's boat, where he tells him to mind his own business and reinforces the message by grabbing the man by his testicles. Tony and Irina make a hasty escape before the Russian's wife alerts the police.

While visiting Hesh Rabkin, Tony regales him with the story and confesses to having episodes where he has passed out. Hesh, however, is not terribly interested and rambles on about other subjects. He does, however, tells Tony that his father, Johnny Boy, suffered panic attacks. Tony is surprised since no one has ever mentioned his father's mental health, but Hesh reassures him that this "condition" only affected Tony's father about twice a year.

Meanwhile, Pussy continues to meet his FBI contact, Agent Skip Lipari, and complains that Tony has not, as of late, let Pussy in on his plans. In addition, Paulie and Johnny Sacks ask Pussy to leave the table when they are about to discuss business.

Trivia

- The episode's title is taken from a song title by Frankie Valli & The Four Seasons.

- It is also a reference to Melfi, who breaks down crying during her therapy with Elliot.

- Although the episode aired fifth, it was the fourth to be produced.

"The Happy Wanderer"

"The Happy Wanderer" is the 19th episode of the HBO original series, The Sopranos. It was the 6th episode for the show's second season. The episode was written by Frank Renzulli and was directed by John Patterson. It originally aired on Sunday February 20, 2000.

Guest Starring

- Lillo Brancato Jr. as Matthew Bevilaqua
- Chris Tardio as Sean Gismonte
- Vince Curatola as Johnny "Sack" Sacrimoni
- Robert Patrick as David Scatino
- John Ventimiglia as Artie Bucco
- Federico Castelluccio as Furio Giunta
- Joseph R. Gannascoli as Vito Spatafore
- Frank Sinatra, Jr. as Himself
- John Hensley as Eric Scatino
- John Fiore as Gigi Cestone
- Lewis J. Stalden as Dr. Ira Fried
- Nicole Burdette as Barbara Soprano Giglione
- Ed Vassalo as Tom Giglione

Synopsis

During College Night at Meadow's school, Tony reunites with an old friend from school, David Scatino, who owns a sporting goods store in Ramsey, New Jersey. Davey casually asks Tony if he can play in the "Executive Game", a high-level poker game established by Tony's father Johnny Boy and uncle Junior in the 1960s, and now resurrected by Tony himself since Junior's house arrest. Tony is wary, however, because Davey has had a compulsive gambling problem, but ultimately lets him join. The following day, Davey begins to owe serious debts after playing at Richie Aprile's small poker game, and falls behind on payments. Richie warns him that missing payments will only cause his debt to escalate faster since missed payments are added to the principal, and bars Davey from the Aprile poker game until he can catch up.

At his therapy session with Dr. Melfi, Tony observes that even though things are going well for him, he still gets angry about everything. Particular venom is directed at "happy wanderers"--people walking down the street with a smile and a happy manner--because "they always walk around with a clear head". Tony, on the other hand, cannot stave off depression and anger even when everything is going well. He mourns the death of his brother-in-law's father, Tom Giglione Sr., who fell off a roof while putting up a satellite dish just one day after his retirement. Tony also worries that therapy encourages feelings of victimisation, while his hero Gary Cooper was always resilient. Tony also learns from Uncle Junior that he had another uncle who was mentally disabled and is at a charity home run by the state. Melfi asks Tony if having a retarded family member makes him feel better about coming to therapy. Tony says that it does not.

At Tom Giglione's funeral, Tony becomes angry when Livia arrives, saying she is dead to him. He also is infuriated when she goes to one of Meadow's performances for school.

Before the card game, Christopher tells Matt and Sean what to expect. Furio has arranged for the game to be held at the Teitleman motel, and when Hillel Teitleman complains about hosting such a criminal activity, Furio reminds him that he has been known to use the services of mob-provided prostitutes, and in the past has requested favors of the mafia which they have willingly delivered. At the card game, the players include Frank Sinatra, Jr., Johnny Sack, Silvio, and Dr. Ira Fried, who specializes in penile implants. Tony is surprised when Davey Scatino arrives and tries to dissuade him from joining, but Davey insists. Come morning, Davey owes Tony $45,000. Richie then visits the motel room and tries to choke Davey for entering an Executive Game when he still owes Richie thousands of dollars. Tony breaks up the fight and takes Richie outside. Richie tells Tony that Davey already owes him $8,000. But because he caused a scene and threatened a player, Tony tells Richie that Davey will pay his debt first and then Richie's. Davey fails to come up with the money for Tony, who finds him at his office and smacks him around a bit to put some fear into him.

Desperate, Davey turns to fellow friend Artie Bucco for a loan, but Artie declines.

As partial payment, Dave gives his son Eric's SUV to Tony, who then gives the car to Meadow. Meadow soon realizes that the car belonged to her classmate Eric and refuses to take it. Tony, however, tells her that he is justified in taking it, and that Meadow needs to either accept what he provides or leave. Eric too has a problem with the arrangement as he is not prepared to pay for his father's losses with his own SUV and feels that the situation is unjust. When they meet later that night to perform a duet with Meadow at their school's cabaret night, he tells Meadow to "make" Tony give his SUV back. Meadow replies that she can't force her dad to do anything, let alone give back an SUV when it's Dave's fault he got in over his head. Eric then drops out minutes before their scheduled performance, saying "fuck you, fuck your gangster father and fuck this." As the show begins, an announcer alerts a program change in the second act, as Meadow will be performing alone. Carmela is surprised, but happy that Meadow will have a solo performance for her college application, while Tony seems recalcitrant and unapologetic for whatever impact he has had on the Scatinos and their friendship with his own family.

First Appearances

- Vito Spatafore, Richie Aprile's nephew who is in his crew as well.

Hits

- Tom Giglione, Sr., Tony's brother-in-law Tom's father who died after falling off a roof.

Symbolism and Thematic Elements

- Once again, Tony has trouble separating his mob life from his family life, and once again, his children are directly affected.

Trivia

- The episode's title is that of a "happy wanderer", a type of person that walks around with no worries in the world, which Tony despises.

- The episode title is also a song of the same name by Frankie Yankovic which is played during the end credits.

- The Executive Game's dealer, "Sunshine", is played by director Paul Mazursky. He would return to deal at Eugene Pontecorvo's poker game in the episode "Amour Fou".

"D-Girl"

"D-Girl" is the 20th episode of the HBO original series, The Sopranos. It was the 7th episode for the show's second season. The episode was written by Todd A. Kessler and was directed by Allen Coulter. It originally aired on Sunday February 27, 2000.

Guest Starring

- Alicia Witt as Amy Safir
- Jon Favreau as Himself
- Sandra Bernhard as Herself
- Janeane Garofalo as Herself
- Federico Castelluccio as Furio Giunta
- Toni Kalem as Angie Bonpensiero
- Louis Lombardi as Agent Skip Lipari
- Frank Pando as Agent Grasso
- Dominic Fumusa as Gregory Moltisanti
- Steve Porcelli as Matt Bonpensiero

Synopsis

A.J., while out joyriding without a license in Carmela's car, hits a truck, leaving a few scratches and a broken rearview mirror. As Carmela attempts to drive out of the garage, the mirror falls off and he is busted. Carmela and Tony then sit A.J. down and lecture him on how he could have killed the people in the car. A.J. is unmoved, however, as he feels that "death just shows the absolute absurdity of life". Appalled, Tony and Carmela ask how he possibly could have been exposed to such an idea, and A.J. explains a devotion to Jean-Paul Sartre. He follows this with a request to not be confirmed because there is no God. Tony brings this up in therapy. He believes it is not normal to question one's faith, but Melfi thinks that existentialist concerns are a natural part of adolescence that was repressed by his parents. Melfi then asks Tony how his relationship with Livia is taking a toll on the children, seeing as how he has publicly and vociferously insisted that his mother is effectively dead to him. Tony does not answer.

Tony turns to Pussy for guidance on A.J., since he is both his godfather and confirmation sponsor. Pussy then takes A.J. and his own college-age son, Matt, to the batting cages where Matt explains that Nietzsche and some of his colleagues were often mentally disturbed or lacking integrity, and advises AJ to study earlier, non-nihilistic philosophy. A.J. explains that he isn't an aetheist; he merely believes God is dead. He is then directed to Livia for some wisdom and guidance. When he tells her how he got in trouble, Livia concurs that life is meaningless and lonely and that everyone is destined to "die in their own arms", which hardly provides useful insight.

Meanwhile, Pussy is forced by the FBI to cooperate and wear a wire while at the confirmation ceremony and party afterward. Hours before the ceremony, Pussy shaves his chest and is repeatedly asked by his wife Angie if she can come in the bathroom. Pussy tries to stop her, and as she opens the door she throws the mirror at him. As he is about to strike her, Matt breaks up the fight. As Pussy gets up, Matt spots blood on his father's chest.

After the ceremony, A.J. is caught smoking pot with a few cousins in the garage, and retreats to his room. Pussy follows him and tells him that his father is a good man, and goes on to regale him with the story of his deceased sister, and how Tony stayed with her in the hospital until her death. After Pussy hugs A.J., the wires on his chest are disturbed and the FBI's reception becomes troublesome. A.J. then goes back downstairs to the party where the family gathers for a picture. When Tony asks where the godfather is, Pussy is shown in the bathroom sobbing.

Later, while having dinner with his cousin Greg and Greg's fiancee, Amy, Chris and Adriana are invited to come on the set of the film they are shooting. Adriana tells Christopher that she believes in him, and has saved a copy of the script he had previously tried to destroy. Christopher goes to the set alone and sits in on a film shoot starring Janeane Garafalo and Sandra Bernhard. When Janeane objects to the word "bitch" in the script, the director has difficulty finding an appropriate word as substitute. Christopher suggests "pucchiaca", Italian for "cunt", which the cast and crew seem enthusiastic about.

Earlier, over lunch, Christopher discusses his screenplay with Jon and Amy, and tells a story about a homophobic mobster's encounter with a transsexual. Christopher soon becomes very close with Amy and they begin seeing each other having a sexual relationship. Adriana, however, has no idea, and is still waiting for Christopher to propose. Christopher storms out of a restaurant when Adriana continues to pressure him, going to Amy's house with the excuse that he was "in the neighborhood." The next morning, Amy wants to come clean to her fiance. Christopher warns her not to, but is soon distracted when he happens upon Jon Favreau's screenplay. While reading the draft, Christopher learns that Jon used the story he had told him. Irate, Christopher searches for Favreau, but he has already returned to L.A. When Christopher approaches Amy, she adopts a cold, businesslike attitude, saying that the studio has lost interest in mob films. Christopher denounces her as a "fucking D-girl", and Amy reminds him that she is a VP, not a D-girl, before storming off.

At the confirmation party, Tony gives Christopher an ultimatum: in ten minutes Christopher is either to make a commitment to the mob life and seek no other distractions, or to continue with his own life. If he chooses the latter, Tony will never want to see him again. Christopher thinks about this on the back steps of Tony's house and then re-enters, pledging his loyalty and respect, as a distraught Pussy continues to weep in the bathroom.

Trivia

- The episode's title is a shortened title for "development girl" used mostly in the film and television industry. Christopher calls Amy this when she spurns him, which she takes as an insult.

- In a Season 6 episode, (Live Free or Die) Hugh de Angelis calls Carmela "Sandra Bernhard" an actress who appeared as herself in this episode.

"Full Leather Jacket"

"Full Leather Jacket" is the 21st episode of the HBO original series, The Sopranos. It was the 8th episode for the show's second season. The episode was written by Robin Green & Mitchell Burgess and was directed by Allen Coulter. It originally aired on Sunday March 5, 2000.

Guest Starring

- Lillo Brancato Jr. as Matthew Bevilaqua
- Chris Tardio as Sean Gismonte
- Saundra Santiago as Jeannie Cusamano and Joan O'Connell
- Steve R. Schirripa as Bobby "Bacala" Baccalieri
- Federico Castelluccio as Furio Giunta
- Joseph R. Gannascoli as Vito Spatafore
- Paul Herman as Peter "Beansie" Gaeta
- Tom Alderige as Hugh De Angelis
- Suzanne Shepherd as Mary De Angelis
- Patty McCormack as Liz La Cerva

Synopsis

Matt Bevilaqua and Sean Gismonte begin working extensively with Christopher, perhaps demonstrating a little too much enthusiasm about moving up in the criminal organization. They also visit Richie, introduce themselves, and listen to him make fun of Christopher and his large proboscis. At the Bada Bing, Matt and Sean try introduce themselves to Tony in the bathroom but are nervous and get into too much detail about their job with Chris. Instead of impressing Tony, this has the opposite effect, and Tony calls Sean a "shit-eating twat" since he did not take precautions about wiretaps before detailing his enthusiasm for illegal activities.

Matt and Sean realize they are small fish in a big pond full of big fish when Furio comes for Tony's 10 percent "cut" and adds another thousand dollars for himself. Later while waiting for Christopher, Matt suggests they take drastic measures in order to be recognized. As Christopher exits the Skyway's Diner in Kearny, he is ambushed by Matt and Sean and shot 3 times. Christopher, however, has time to pull his own weapon and Sean is killed. Matt manages to get away and escape to Richie's hangout, where he confesses to Richie and says that they did it to prove themselves to him. Richie is enraged and chases Matt with a baseball batt.

Meanwhile Carmela and Tony are concerned that Meadow might go to Berkeley. Carmela tells Tony that in order to get ahead with college admissions, one has to "know someone or donate 5 buildings". Carmela then remembers that her neighbor's twin sister Joan is an alumna of Georgetown University. When Jeannie fails to persuade Joan to write a letter of recommendation on Meadow's behalf, Carmela gives her a ricotta pie and a folder of high school transcripts and teacher recommendations. Joan initially declines, but then Carmela tells her she is not asking, she "wants" the letter of recommendation. Joan asks Carmela if she is threatening her and Carmela insists she is not. Later, Jeannie Cusamano visits Carmela to bring back the plate and to inform her that Joan has looked at Meadow's transcripts and has written a letter of recommendation. Carmela asks for a copy, and Jeannie promises she will give her one.

Before he was shot, Christopher went to Adriana's mother's home where he apologizes for abandoning her at the restaurant weeks ago, and for abusing her. Christopher then proposes to Adriana, and Adriana says yes. Her mother, however, warns Adriana that if she gets hurt again "this door is closed to you".

Silvio and Paulie pressure Richie Aprile to help Beansie Gaeta cope better with being in a wheelchair. Richie refuses at first however after hearing that the request was from Tony, Richie sends both Vito and an associate over to make sure that Beansie's house is renovated to be more wheelchair accessible. Tony then hears from Gia Gaeta that the job was half finished, and when confronted, Richie says they will complete the work eventually but right now, Richie is currently re-renovating Livia Soprano's home. As a sign of friendship, Richie gives Tony a leather jacket from the '70s that was taken off of tough guy Rocco Di Meo. Tony hesistatingly accepts the gesture but then passes the gift to his cleaning woman Liliana's husband, a mechanical engineer from Poland. Richie sees Liliana's husband wearing the jacket when he drops off some food he had made for Carmela, and is depressed and angered.

Soon after hearing of Christopher's shooting, Tony and the remainder of the family arrive at the hospital. As Christopher lies in a coma, Tony sits in a chair and asks "how could this have happened?"

Hits

- Sean Gismonte, shot in defense by Christopher.

Trivia

- The episode's title is a play on the 1987 film, Full Metal Jacket where that phrase refers to metal jacketed bullets

- Saundra Santiago plays a dual role portraying twin sisters, Jeannie Cusamano and Joannie O'Connell in this episode.

- Although the episode aired eighth, it was the seventh to be produced.

- Unlike the other episodes, there is no song at the conclusion of the episode. Instead all that is heard is the sound of Christopher's ventilator and the Electrocardiogram machine.

"From Where to Eternity"

"From Where to Eternity" is the 22nd episode of the HBO original series, the Sopranos. It was the ninth episode for the show's second season. The episode was written by Michael Imperioli and directed by Henry J. Bronchtein. It originally aired on Sunday March 12, 2000.

Guest Starring

- Lillo Brancato Jr. as Matthew Bevilaqua
- Jerry Adler as Hesh Rabkin
- Louis Lombardi as Agent Skip Lipari
- Peter Bogdanovich as Dr. Eliott Kupferberg
- Maureen Van Zandt as Gabriella Dante
- Judy Reyes as Paulie's Girlfriend

Synopsis

Christopher clings to life in a hospital ICU. During the night his heart stops and though he is clinically dead for over a minute, the medical team manages to revive him. Fearing for his life, Carmela prays that Christopher will recover and "see the light". When he is conscious, he asks to see Paulie and Tony. He tells them of a trip he made to hell where he saw Brendan Filone and Mikey Palmice in an Irish bar and they sent the message "three o'clock" to Tony and Paulie.

Tony doesn't worry much about Christopher's story, but Paulie becomes obsessed with the message. Paulie is scared on a regular basis at 3am and has nightmares that wake his girlfriend's children. Eventually, he goes to a psychic who claims to see the ghosts of the men that Paulie killed, following his every step. Believing his donations to a church should have prevented him from being haunted, Paulie takes out his frustration on a chain-smoking priest, telling him he feels that the Church has forsaken him and that he won't be giving any more donations.

Meanwhile Carmela learns from Gabriella that an associate of the Soprano family, Ralphie Rotaldo, just had a baby with his mistress. Carmela then asks that Tony have a vasectomy since she knows that he still sees women on the side. Tony tries to shake off the accusation since he allegedly broke up with Irina months ago. Carmela then reminds him of the shame that a "bastard-child" would do to her family. Tony does not wish to discuss it so Carmela takes a pillow and prepares to sleep downstairs. Adding to Carmela's anger is the fact that Tony lied to her about Christopher's vision of the afterlife, telling her that Christopher had been in heaven while Christopher told her he was in Hell. Tony is further subjected to Carmela's anger when he criticizes his "only male heir," his son A.J., after he spills food on the floor accidentally. Soon after Tony apologizes to A.J., Tony agrees to have his vasectomy if Carmela insists. Carmela says no, she doesnt insist on a vasectomy, but that she wants him to be pure and to be hers. They then make love.

Pussy is afraid that Tony knows he has been working with the FBI, so at the advice of his FBI contact Pussy tries to "make Tony love him again." Pussy tries to regain his trust by hunting down Matt Bevilaqua. When he gets the information as to his whereabouts, Pussy calls Tony and the two execute Matt, riddling his body with bullets.

Hits

- Matthew Bevilaqua, repeatedly shot execution style by Tony and Pussy in revenge for Christopher's shooting

Trivia

- The episode's title is a play on the 1953 film, From Here to Eternity. It refers to Christopher having a trip to the afterlife and not knowing whether it was purgatory or hell.

- The song "My Lover's Prayer" by Otis Redding is played throughout the episode.

- Although the episode aired ninth, it was the eighth to be produced.

- In his dream, Christopher describes that Mikey Palmice and Brendan Filone claimed that the time of Three o'clock will be important in the lives of Tony and Paulie.

Since then, several important events have taken place at Three o'clock and it has become a key recurring symbol.

- This was the first episode written by Michael Imperioli

- *Carmela's Prayer: *Gentle and merciful lord Jesus, I want to speak to you now with an open heart, with an honest heart. Tonight I ask you to take my sins and the sins of my family into your merciful heart. We have chosen this life in full awareness of the consequences of our sins. I know that Christopher's life is in your hands... And his fate is your will. I ask you humbly to spare him. And if it is your will to spare him, I ask that you deliver him from blindness and grant him vision. And through this vision may he see your love... And gain the strength to carry on in service to your mercy. In the name of the Father, the Son, and the Holy Spirit, Amen.

"Bust Out"

"Bust Out" is the 23rd episode of the HBO original series, The Sopranos. It was the tenth episode for the show's second season. The episode was written by Frank Renzulli and Robin Green & Mitchell Burgess and directed by John Patterson. It originally aired on Sunday March 19, 2000.

Guest Starring

- The police locate an eyewitness to the Bevilaqua killing who identifies Tony from a book of suspect photos. He didn't get a good look at Pussy, but describes the second man as "heavyset". Tony, frantic with worry, decides to leave town until the witness is dealt with, giving a sports bag full of cash to his lawyer, Neil Mink, to provide for his family. Luckily for Tony, the witness realises via a newspaper article that the murder relates to the Mafia, and contacts the police department to retract his statement and rescind his interest in offering testimony.

- Tony and Richie, then, continue to siphon money out of Davey's store, ordering bottled water, coolers, airline tickets and sneakers on the store's credit and selling the stuff on the street. They inform Davey that this will continue unless he is able to pay the money he owes them.

- Davey is, to say the least, stressed out and is shown in his basement pointing a pistol into his mouth. When his wife enters the room he hides the pistol in the ceiling tiles and claims to be fixing a light. Later, his wife and Carmela have lunch at Nuovo Vesuvio and she confides in Carmela that she is worried about Davey's gambling, mentioning that the sporting goods store is in her name. Artie Bucco serves them the water that Tony had Davey order, mentioning that he got a great deal on the price.

- Unhappy with the cut he is getting from Davey's store and the deal he has with Barone Sanitation, Richie discusses with Junior the possibility of getting rid of Tony. When Junior scolds him, Richie reminds him of his own plan to kill Tony the previous year.

- Carmela is attracted to a new handyman, the brother of Davey's wife, who is a widower. He and Carmela kiss, and then she invites him over for a discussion and meal. Later on, he learns of Tony's involvement with his brother-in-law, Davey, and sends a worker to meet her instead of arriving himself.

- Tony tries to get closer to A.J. and Meadow, but his efforts are in vain.

Trivia

- A "bust out" is a common tactic in the organized crime world where a business's assets and lines of credit are exploited and exhausted to the point of bankruptcy. Richie and Tony profit from busting out Davey Scatino's sporting goods store in this episode.

- When asked by Davey why he let him get into debt, Tony tells him it was because he knew he had the store and other assets he could take, and saw an opportunity for profit. In a similar situation with Artie in Season Four, Tony reacts angrily when Artie accuses him of that line of thinking.

- Cast members David Proval and Aida Turturro expressed concerns about filming their sex scene in this episode.

- The song playing at the end of the episode is "Wheel in the Sky" by Journey.

"House Arrest"

"House Arrest" is the 24th episode of the HBO original series, The Sopranos. It was the 11th episode for the show's second season. The episode was written by Terence Winter and was directed by Tim Van Patten. It originally aired on Sunday March 25, 2000.

Guest Starring

- Jerry Adler as Hesh Rabkin
- Sharon Angela as Rosalie Aprile
- Toni Kalem as Angie Bonpensiero
- Steve R. Schirripa as Bobby "Bacala" Baccalieri
- Federico Castelluccio as Furio Giunta
- Mary Louise Wilson as Catherine Romano
- David Marguilles as Neil Mink
- Peter Bogdanovich as Dr. Elliot Kupferberg
- Matt Servitto as Agent Dwight Harris
- Matthew Sussman as Dr. Schreck
- Maureen Van Zandt as Gabriella Dante
- Joe Lisi as Dick Barone

Synopsis

Uncle Junior and Richie Aprile begin earing money on the side by selling cocaine on the Barone Sanitation garbage routes. When Tony learns about this, he warns Richie to stop, saying that drug sales will only pull FBI and DEA attention onto the family's business ties to the garbage industry. When informed of his nephew's decision, Uncle Junior decides to go against Tony since the cocaine has been a good and steady source of income for him.

Tony's attorney, Neil Mink, cautions Tony that the FBI is trying to figure out ways to indict him after the failed accusation with the Matthew Bevilaqua murder. Neil suggests that Tony begin reporting to Barone Sanitation in order to fulfill his official job as a waste management consultant. Tony does so but becomes increasingly bored and restless on the job as the days drag on, passing his time there by having sex with the receptionist and making a company pool for sports. At a company banquet, Tony suffers an anxiety attack and is rushed to the hospital. After he discovers a rash on his arm, aggravated by stress, he accuses Melfi of giving him poor treatment and ergo causing his relapse. Melfi in turn begins drinking between sessions, and at a meal with her son Jason, she drinks too much and rudely asks a woman at the table next to them to put out her cigarette. When she refuses, Melfi puts the cigarette out herself and is asked to leave.

Meanwhile, Uncle Junior goes to Dr. Schreck after he has difficulty breathing. Dr. Schreck recommends that he breathe using a special mask to help him with his excessive snoring and to take pressure off of his heart. As he leaves the hospital, a court officer places an electronic bracelet on Junior's leg. In the hallway, Junior reunites with an the widow of a close friend,

Catherine Romano. He tries to cover up the legal troubles he's facing, and is quickly forced to make excuses when Catherine drops by with a tray of manicotti and suggests they go out. Finally, he comes clean with her about the condistions of his house arrest, and to his relief, Catherine understands and tells Junior that she enjoys spending time with him despite the fact that he got into trouble. Catherine demonstrates her affection for Junior by massaging him and helping him put on his mask at night.

Tony decides to return to work at Satriale's after being stifled by boredom at Barone Sanitation. Tony is welcomed back to work by his underlings, as well as Agent Harris who is in the neighborhood to introduce his new partner. Tony and his crew idly relax around the store, but are soon occupied when a neighborhood street racer crashes his car outside.

"The Knight in White Satin Armor"

"The Knight in White Satin Armor" is the 25th episode of the HBO original series, The Sopranos. It was the 12th episode for the show's second season. The episode was written by Robin Green & Mitchell Burgess and directed by Allen Coulter. It originally aired on Sunday April 2, 2000.

It was nominated for the 2000 Emmy Award for Outstanding Writing for a Drama Series.

Guest Starring

- Jason Cerbone as Jackie Aprile, Jr.
- Louis Lombardi as Agent Skip Lipari
- Steven R. Schirripa as Bobby "Bacala" Baccalieri
- Joe Penny as Victor Musto
- Joe Lisi as Dick Barone
- Richard Maldone as Albert Barese
- Andy Blankenbuehler as "Little Ricky" Aprile
- Oksana Lada as Irina Peltsin
- Alla Klikuoa Schaffer as Svetlana Kirenklo
- Sharon Angela as Rosalie Aprile
- Maureen Van Zandt as Gabriella Dante
- Richard Portnow as Harold Melvoin

Synopsis

After Janice tells Tony that she knows about his Russian girlfriend, Tony attempts to break it off with Irina, and insists to Irina that she deserves better than remaining his mistress. Irina is not really with the program, telling Tony she loves him and will commit suicide if he leaves her, but he walks out. Tony later receives a call from Irina's cousin Svetlana, who tells him that Irina made good on her promise and washed down a bottle of pills with a bottle of vodka. Tony then discusses Irina with Dr. Melfi and asks if she can find her a suitable therapist. Melfi refuses, feeling that this will make her too involved in Tony's crime life. He turns to Carmela and tells her what is going on, but Carmela she becomes irate, screaming "you're putting me in a position where I am feeling sorry for a whore who fucks you!". To make the problem go away, Tony sends Silvio to Irina's house with a parting gift of $75,000, and along with Svetlana, he persuades her to move on with her life.

At Richie and Janice's engagement party hosted by Tony, Richie professes his love for Janice and his gratitude that he is entering a great family. Carmela escapes to the kitchen where she cries uncontrollably. The following day, she visits Vic Musto at a paint store where she thanks him for not showing up to their scheduled lunch date since she would have done things she would have regretted.

Pussy, as an FBI informant, wears a wire to Richie and Janice's engagement party and then gives them useful information about stolen airline tickets, and Tony's gambling situation with Davey Scatino. However, Pussy begins to develop an unrealistic image of his new role. When he learns that Christopher is planning a to hijack a shipment of Pokemon cards, Pussy attempts to conduct his own surveillance and follow them to the heist, but winds up in a car accident. At the hospital, his handler Skip Lipari reminds Pussy that he is not a government employee and that he should focus his energy on providing information about Tony, and only on providing information about Tony.

Richie's resentment of Tony grows when he is again ordered to stop making money on the side via selling cocaine on his garbage truck routes. Later, Janice contributes to his resentment when she tells him that Tony refuses to have his children around him since he ran over Beansie, and believes he is a bad influence. Richie approaches Uncle Junior and suggests having Tony killed, but Junior is not terribly interested in this plan of action, mindful of his own failure to do so last year, and his reconciliation with Tony in the months since. When Richie insists that he can muster support from other dissatisfied crews such as the Bareses, Junior comes around; but once Richie departs, Junior concludes that having Richie in power would ultimately cause him more trouble.

Meanwhile, Richie visits Albert Barese, acting capo of the Barese crew since his cousin Larry Boy's indictment, to try to win his allegiance, but Albert refuses to hit Tony. Richie returns home to dinner with Janice, and expresses disgust for his son Richard Jr.'s career path as a ballroom dancer. When Janice takes offense, saying she does not care if "Little Ricky" is gay, he punches her in the mouth and then asks her "what, are you going to cry now?". Janice responds by getting a gun from the other room and shooting Richie twice in the chest, and he dies right there on the floor. Panicking, Janice calls Tony to take care of the body which he does by enlisting the help of Christopher and Furio, who put the body in a meat grinder. Tony then gives Janice a bus ticket to Seattle and they part ways.

Tony hints to Carmela that Richie will never come back, and though she is somewhat shocked, she somehow segues this news into telling Tony that she and Rosalie Aprile will be traveling to Rome to see Pope John Paul II. Carmela asks that Tony be a "chauffeur" to A.J. and to find Meadow a suitable tennis camp while she is away, snidely suggesting that she "just might commit suicide" unless he agrees.

First Appearances

- Jackie Aprile, Jr., Richie's nephew and son of Rosalie Aprile and the late Jackie Aprile, Sr..

- Albert Barese, Acting capo of the Barese crew while his cousin Larry Boy Barese is under indictment.

- Svetlana Kirilenko, the cousin of Tony's comare Irina who will later play a larger role

Hits

- Richie Aprile, shot by Janice after he punched her in the mouth

Trivia

- The episode's title is a quote made by Irina about her cousin Svetlana's fiancee Bill who treats her the way she should be treated.

- The song "I Saved The World Today" by Eurythmics is played over the credits, and throughout the episode.

- The scene where Richie punches Janice was filmed without stunt doubles.

"Funhouse"

"Funhouse" is the 26th episode of the HBO original series, The Sopranos. It was the final episode for the show's second season. The episode was written by David Chase and Todd A. Kessler and was directed by John Patterson. It originally aired on Sunday, April 9, 2000.

It was nominated for the 2000 Emmy Award for Outstanding Writing for a Drama Series.

Guest Starring

- Robert Patrick as David Scatino
- John Ventimiglia as Artie Bucco
- Kathrine Narducci as Charmaine Bucco
- Dan Grimaldi as Patsy Parisi and Philly "Spoons" Parisi
- Peter Bogdanovich as Dr. Elliot Kupferberg
- Toni Kalem as Angie Bonpensiero
- Jerry Adler as Hesh Rabkin
- Sofia Milos as Annalisa Zucca
- Frank Pellegrino as Bureau Chief Frank Cubitoso
- Matt Servitto as Agent Harris
- Suzanne Shepherd as Mary De Angelis
- Tom Alderige as Hugh De Angelis
- David Marguiles as Neil Mink
- Nicole Burdette as Barbara Soprano Giglione

- Barbara Andres as Aunt Quintina
- Maureen Van Zandt as Gabriella Dante
- John Fiore as Gigi Cestone

Synopsis

Shortly after Janice leaves for Seattle, Tony and his younger sister Barbara try to talk to Livia about her living siutation. When Livia refuses to move in either with Tony and Carmela or Barbara, Tony hands Livia two airline tickets to Arizona (one for herself and for her sister Quintina) and warns her to leave for good.

Later, Tony discusses a calling card credit scheme with Silvio Dante and Big Pussy Bonpiensero at Artie Bucco's restaurant, immediately after eating at an Indian restaurant. During the night, Tony dreams that he is walking on the boardwalk in Asbury Park and meets up with Paulie, Silvio, Christopher, Pussy and Philly "Spoons". In the dream, Tony has six months to live from a terminal illness. Silvio hands Tony a bottle of gasoline which and Tony uses it for self-immolation. Tony then quickly awakes to a vicious bout of diarrhea and vomiting.

The following morning, Carmela contacts Artie and tells him that Tony has food poisoning from eating at his restauarant. When Artie arrives at the Soprano home, he quickly learns that Tony ate at an Indian restaurant which could have also caused sickness. Eventually, Artie calls up Big Pussy to see if he is sick as well. Tony then goes into a delirium after receiving a house call from Doctor Cusamano and eventually falls asleep, dreaming about having sex with Dr. Melfi in her office.

At Dr. Melfi's, Tony goes off on a racist rant against Indian people and also rants about against his mother. Tony then refuses to analyze anything or do any real work in this particular session, and tells her of his sex dream with her before he storms out.

Tony has one more dream, involving him speaking to Big Pussy, who has taken the form of a fish. In the morning, Meadow tells her parents she is going to Columbia University. Tony and Silvio later go to Pussy's house, and invite him to go boating with them. Searching Pussy's room, Tony finds proof that Pussy is an FBI informant.

Silvio, Tony and Pussy meet up with Paulie Walnuts at the dock, and they sail out together. On the boat, Tony demands of Pussy to know how long it has been since he "flipped." Pussy finally gives in under the pressure, and claims not to have given any big pieces of information to the Feds, but Tony does not believe him. Silvio excuses himself, claiming to be sick.

Pussy asks for tequila, and Paulie pours Jose Cuervo for Tony and Pussy. Eventually, sad and realizing he is cornered, Pussy asks to not be shot in the face. Then, as he asks to be allowed to sit, Tony, Paulie and Silvio shoot him to death. Together they bind him in chains and throw him over the side of the boat.

Hours later, Carmela receives a phone call from Livia. She is being detained in Airport Security for possessing stolen airline tickets. Within minutes, FBI agents arrive. In actuality an agent has already searched Tony's car and found the stolen tickets. Tony is placed in handcuffs and is taken to FBI offices for questioning, and luckily, after a call to his lawyer, he is released on bail in time for Meadow's graduation the next day.

The following day at Meadow's graduation ceremony, Tony proudly watches his daughter accept her diploma. At the graduation, Tony tells Christopher that he is proposing him to get his button. The episode ends with a montage of Tony's two families celebrating Meadow's graduation, interspersed with the images of the various illegal enterprises that comprise the Soprano business.

Hits

- Salvatore "Big Pussy" Bonpensiero, murdered by Tony, Silvio, and Paulie for being an FBI informant. His body was tossed into the ocean.

Trivia

- In Tony's dream, he is on the boardwalk in Asbury Park, near a funhouse with a wide-eyed clown painted on it.

- The song played throughout the episode is "Thru and Thru" by The Rolling Stones.

- Actor Dan Grimaldi plays both Parisi brothers in this episode.

Index

Al Pacino 33, 45
Arizona 160
Avellino 84
Bada Bing ... 27, 31, 33, 35, 62, 70, 89, 96, 97, 138
Barone Sanitation .. 146, 150, 151, 152
Bowdoin College 48
Camorra family 115
cancer 28, 32, 35, 44
capo .. 54, 66, 80, 91, 121, 156, 157
Casino 14, 51
cocaine 56, 150, 156
Comley Trucking 28, 34
consigliere 11, 32, 121
DiMeo family 12, 43
ducks 13, 19, 20, 123
Ernest Hemingway 67
Essex County 44
FBI . 47, 54, 62, 63, 71, 79, 85, 86, 89, 91, 93, 105, 107, 116, 119, 124, 132, 133, 143, 151, 155, 161, 162
funeral 83, 127
Goodfellas 13, 45, 67
Green Grove 20, 25, 29, 36, 58, 81, 89, 92, 104
Jean-Paul Sartre 132
Jefferson Airplane 59
Lupertazzi crime family ... 66
Masada 35, 38

Massarone Construction 105
Moe Greene 45
Nathaniel Hawthorne 48
New Jersey . 11, 18, 24, 44, 45, 48, 50, 59, 62, 96, 126
New York's Five Families. 54
Nuovo Vesuvio ... 88, 92, 121, 146
panic attack 18, 20, 30, 98
Passaic River 59
payphones 33
police . 44, 63, 66, 80, 90, 110, 123, 145
Prozac 20, 122
Scarface 45
soccer 22, 23, 26, 70
Soprano family 63, 76, 80, 99, 104, 106, 121, 142
speed 27, 28, 36, 47, 85
Tennessee Williams 66
The Godfather 14, 23, 24, 38, 51, 115
The Wizard of Oz 111
therapy 10, 14, 20, 25, 30, 35, 42, 43, 65, 71, 74, 85, 96, 98, 111, 124, 126, 132
Tri Borough 28
Verbum Dei 57
Vessuvio 20
wire .. 48, 50, 80, 88, 107, 132, 155

www.ingramcontent.com/pod-product-compliance
Lightning Source LLC
Chambersburg PA
CBHW031148160426
43193CB00008B/296